Advance Praise for *Game the Plan*

"As the founder and CEO of the company that pioneered on-demand SPM, Chris Cabrera stands out his vision, his experience, and his access to hard data. It takes his unusual combination to inspire his unconventional insight— that gaming can be the source of innovation and motivation, and that the best incentive planners will invite gaming that adds to the bottom line."
—Alan Benson, PhD candidate, MIT Sloan

"The ideas in *Game the Plan* resonate for me both as a business executive and a former pro football player. As evidenced in my own life, the possibility of winning the Super Bowl was enough incentive for me to give all I could by cutting off part of my little finger. The right incentives are powerful motivators and *Game the Plan* explains these ideas brilliantly."
—Ronnie Lott, NFL Hall of Fame 2000 Inductee

"Chris and his team have designed a tool that creates more engaged employees, drives the right behavior, and helps organizations meet their goals. I've seen his principles work firsthand over my own career."
—Steve Cakebread, former CFO, salesforce.com

"This is an easy, fast, and insightful read that delivers far more than even the title promises. While it's fun to read how Chris Cabrera got fired and then competed with his previous employer to build a highly successful company, the real value of this meaningful book leaps at you as the author unveils the many powerful links between human motivation and business performance. A must-read for C-level executives."
—Gerhard Gschwandtner, Founder & CEO, Selling Power

"In *Game the Plan*, Chris Cabrera gives us real-world tips, relevant research, and great examples to better reward our sales producers. Start here to "game the plan" well!"
—David J. Cichelli, Sr. Vice President, The Alexander Group, Inc

"Compensation plans can make or break employee morale and customer satisfaction. Chris Cabrera not only knows all that, but in this book, for the first time, he shows you how to build those plans. They work for employees and drive business with customers. So start reading the book. You'll be really glad you did."

—Paul Greenberg, author, *CRM at the Speed of Light* (4th edition)

"Chris Cabrera challenges everyday thinking and common perceptions about sales incentives and makes you rethink your strategies. If you've thumbed your nose at incentives because you think they create win-lose scenarios, Chris will quickly change your mind. You'll read the last page of this book hoping your reps game the plan."

—Keith Krach, Chairman & CEO, DocuSign

"Chris has written a fantastic book for executives that helps bridge the "sales & finance" chasm of compensation. He has some spot-on tips for helping sales and finance work together. I've always been interested in motivation, so I especially enjoyed his sections on how to treat different generations: Traditionalists, Baby Boomers, Gen X, and Gen Y. Plus, his 'Top 5 Motivation Mistakes' are so true and so common. If you deal with compensation—particularly sales compensation—you need to read this book."

—Aaron Ross, bestselling author of *Predictable Revenue*

"*Game the Plan* is the perfect example of why you should go with the tide instead of against it. There's brilliance in the simplicity of taking the natural tendencies of human behavior and rewarding those who achieve financial results."

—Rodahl Leong-Lyons, VP of Sales–Americas, Hyatt Hotels Corporation

"*Game the Plan* is a must-read. Chris Cabrera shows how to use real-life data to create killer incentive compensation strategies that will transform your enterprise."

—Marc Benioff, Chairman and CEO, salesforce.com

GAME
THE PLAN

EVERY SALES REP'S DREAM;
EVERY CFO'S NIGHTMARE

CHRISTOPHER W. CABRERA

FOUNDER AND CEO OF XACTLY CORPORATION

RIVER GROVE
BOOKS

Published by River Grove Books
Austin, TX
www.rivergrovebooks.com

Distributed by River Grove Books

For ordering information or special discounts for bulk purchases, please contact River Grove Books at PO Box 91869, Austin, TX 78709, 512.891.6100.

Design and composition by Greenleaf Book Group LLC
Cover design by Xactly Corp.

Publisher's Cataloging-In-Publication Data
Cabrera, Christopher W.
   Game the plan : every sales rep's dream, every CFO's nightmare / Christopher W. Cabrera.—1st ed.
      p. ; cm.
   Issued also as an ebook.
   Includes bibliographical references.

   1. Sales personnel—Salaries, etc. 2. Incentives in industry. 3. Compensation management. I. Title.

HF5439.7 .C23 2014
658.3/225   2013954723

Paperback ISBN 978-1-938416-54-5
Ebook ISBN 978-1-938416-55-2
Hardcover ISBN 978-1-938416-74-3

Printed in the United States of America on acid-free paper

14 15 16 17 18 19   1 2 3 4 5 6 7 8 9 10

First Edition

I dedicate this book to my father. He was my mentor and inspiration, and he left us too soon.

CONTENTS

FOREWORD

When Chris Cabrera asked me to write this foreword, I didn't think twice about accepting.

Chris and I first met when I was at the software company Autodesk. He sold me an on-site compensation system that was truly terrible. It created more problems than solutions. (Chris tells his side of the story in the introduction.) A few years later, when I was at salesforce.com, he tried to sell me a new-and-improved version of that same software. Although the headaches caused by the last product were gone, they weren't forgotten. My answer was, unequivocally, "No way."

Although that exchange could have threatened our relationship, it didn't. Despite the fact that I was a finance guy and Chris was a sales guy, we had a lot in common. We both cared deeply about finding the best ways to motivate and incent employees. As two people with vast experience in the area of incentive compensation, we knew the current way of doing things could use some serious improvement. Plus, Chris wanted to know my reasoning. He asked me a simple question that changed the way my organization—and many like it—managed incentive compensation: "Why not?"

So I told him. He listened to me talk about why on-site systems didn't work. He listened to me talk about where current incentive compensation systems fell short, and how I thought they needed to evolve to provide value to today's growing, modern organizations.

Basically, I was describing every CFO's nightmare, which is why I understood the tagline for this book immediately.

Chris listened to me talk about my nightmare. Then, he left with his software, and I went back to using spreadsheets to manage my sales incentive compensation. I knew my system was far from perfect—that there had to be a better way of doing things—but at the time, it was really the only option left to me. I simply wasn't willing to consider using an on-site system. Instead, I would sit tight and wait for something better to come along.

And it did, a few months later, when Chris sat across from me again. This time he was CEO of the newly minted Xactly, and he was excited to tell me about a brand-new incentive compensation system he and his team had created: a cloud-based, software as a service (SaaS) incentive compensation system that promised to meet all of my expectations, and more.

I was excited, not to mention a bit honored, to hear that my feedback a few months before had motivated him to start the company.

As I mentioned above, I'm a finance guy and Chris is a sales guy. I work with a lot of salespeople, and it often feels like we're living on two different planets. Sales leaders will do some crazy expensive stuff to increase sales. Finance people like me are constantly trying to rein things in. But the more I listened to Chris, the more excited I became, because I realized he had created a product that would finally allow sales and finance people to speak the same language. This product would give organizations like mine the clear, hard data they needed to make decisions that both Sales and Finance could get behind.

Chris had listened to me, and after listening to him, I was eager to become a customer.

At the time, salesforce.com was a rapidly growing organization, and as we added more and more sales reps to keep up with demand, we realized we didn't necessarily have the administrative staff to keep up with commission work. Our staff was spending three or four days each month trying to get commissions paid on a timely basis, but we still fell behind. On average, it took about sixty days for us to pay sales reps, and many of the checks we cut contained spreadsheet-based human and mathematical errors.

But when we started using the product that Chris and his team had developed at Xactly, everything changed. Soon we were cutting checks in a timely and accurate manner at the end of every month. No matter how many additional sales reps we brought on board, we didn't need to hire additional staff to manage their commissions.

One of the best things about our new incentive compensation system was its impact on engagement and motivation. We all know that sales reps are independent people who thrive on controlling their own destinies. The visibility the system provided enabled reps to get real-time info about how they were performing and what their checks would look like. A rep could look at his stats every day—every hour, if he preferred to—and figure out exactly what needed to be done to increase sales. The software gave reps their independence, enabling them to see what they were doing and better manage the consequences of their actions.

Another terrific benefit: Sales and finance teams struggle less. The hard data gleaned from the software helped guide discussions, leading both teams to speak the same language and support each other. You just can't argue with data! This was a big win for our sales team, a big win for our finance team, and a big win for Salesforce in general.

As far as I'm concerned, no one is more qualified than Chris to write a book on motivating and engaging not just your sales force but also your entire workforce. I've seen his principles work firsthand over my own career, from salesforce.com to Pandora to D-Wave Systems. He doesn't just talk up an idea. He and his team actually use what researchers have learned about the science of motivation to walk the walk. Having been to hell and back, so to speak, in the on-premises software world, they've designed a SaaS tool that creates more engaged employees, drives the right behavior, and helps organizations meet their goals. And I think they've just scratched the surface.

In this book, Chris not only shares what he has spent years learning about motivation and engagement but also shows you how to use data to motivate and incent your sales reps, create collaboration between Sales and Finance, and forecast the future so you can make critical decisions that help your organization succeed. What kind of amazing results could you get if you used industry-trended benchmark data and insights into your own organization's performance to plug into your people power?

Steve Cakebread
Autumn 2013

ACKNOWLEDGMENTS

Writing a book about the core principles that not only first motivated Satish and me to found Xactly Corporation in 2005 but also sustained us along the way has been on my bucket list for years. Time isn't always easy for me to wrangle. But thanks to my dynamite team, I've finally written *Game the Plan*, the book I'd only dreamed of writing until now.

To my family: Marla, my wife, and Alexa and Cole, my children. Because of your love and support, I already enjoy the best win-win there is.

To Satish: Without you, the technology piece that supports the main messages of this book would not have been possible.

To my board, investors, and mentors: I am largely a product of your generous investment in me. Awards that I've been fortunate to win I earned in no small part because of your guidance.

And finally, to Michael Greeves, Caitlin Roberson, and the

Clear Content Marketing team: You got it right from the beginning, and the amount of heavy lifting you did was truly amazing.

To everyone at Xactly, and to others who've inspired me along the way: Thank you; I am extremely grateful. Together, we are transforming the win-lose paradigm of motivation that has dominated the corporate office for too long into an innovative one: a prototype of a win-win.

Now, let's get to work on the sequel!

GAMING THE PLAN IS FAIR GAME

Whether you are a sales rep just beginning your career or a seasoned CFO, you probably picked up this book because you were intrigued by its title. If you are that sales rep, "gaming the plan"—the practice of finding loopholes in your company's incentive plan to maximize earnings—is your ultimate dream. But if you are that CFO, it's your worst nightmare.

The following three scenarios explain what I mean:

- **Scenario "No Fun" One.** A rep who earns commissions based on top-line sales revenue slashes prices and undercuts competitors just so he can close as many deals as possible. This rep walks away with a bundle in commissions while the organization loses money.

- **Scenario "Terrible" Two.** A rep with a unit-based incentive plan that does not prioritize products sells the easiest products: discounted, bargain-priced products the company has decided to sell at a loss. This rep takes home a healthy commission check while the company loses money.

- **Scenario "Triple Threat" Three.** A rep with a monthly objective and achievement bonus maximizes her commissions by selling hard one month and relaxing the next. This rep makes the most money doing half the work she is capable of while the organization misses out on additional profits.

All of these are win-lose situations: The rep wins; the company loses. As a result, many company leaders become obsessed with this question: What can we do to *stop reps from gaming the plan*? They spend lots of time trying to stay one step ahead of their reps, imagining all of the nefarious ways in which they might game the incentive plan in the hope of coming up with measures to stop them. As a result, many companies decide to significantly reduce incentives or to walk away from them entirely.

But I have another idea: Let your reps game the heck out of your plan.

The simple fact is this: Within five minutes of your announcing an incentive, your top performers will quickly find ways to game the system to maximize their commissions by any means possible. And that's exactly what you should want them to do, because if reps are gaming, it means they are actually trying to achieve the goals you have set.

But if gaming results is their win and your loss, then you've written a bad compensation plan. Don't blame the reps for that; blame the people who wrote the plan. Then, write a different plan, knowing your reps will exploit it. Don't just allow reps to game the plan, give them obvious ways in which to do so. Help them out.

As long as the plan aligns the employees' self-interest with the company's self-interest, you've got nothing to be afraid of. Reps may find ways to squeeze every last dime out of your incentive compensation plan, but with your new plan in place, it will only be to the organization's benefit. A good incentive compensation plan creates a win-win situation in which the more ways a rep can find to make money, the more the organization earns.

People are motivated by self-interest. You'll never get a rep to put the interests of your company ahead of his own. In fact, many studies have shown that one of the greatest motivators of all is the need to feel safe and secure. But I learned that lesson the hard way: I was canned.

THE INCENTIVE OF GETTING FIRED

Before I founded Xactly Corporation in 2005 with Satish Palvai, I worked at a software company that is now one of Xactly's biggest competitors in the incentive compensation market. People often ask what compelled me to leave that organization and start my own company. After all, I was SVP of operations at the time.

I always tell them the truth: I was fired.

You might wonder why I'm beginning a book about sales incentive compensation with a story about getting sacked. The way I see it, the story of how I left that particular company illustrates, on a deep level, what incentives are and why they are so powerful.

My exit actually had its start in October 2003, when my employer went public. Shortly after that, given the unpredictable nature of the large software license on-prem business model, the CEO was ousted from the company. There we were, leaderless and just six months into being a public company. I wasn't happy to see him go—to this day, he's still a close friend—but after accepting the fact of his departure, I must admit I had grand illusions of taking his place! There I was, thinking I was the No. 2 guy. My teams had been largely responsible for building the company from zero to a $100 million run rate, and I expected to cruise right into filling the CEO vacancy. It was just a matter of time, I thought, before the board figured it out. Turns out, the board had its own agenda. They promoted a relatively new, conservative board member to act as interim CEO.

For the next six months, I attempted to ingratiate myself with this leader. I was passionate about the company and all I'd contributed to its success in the previous seven years. But our relationship was challenging. Our styles were very different, for one, and I viewed his firm ideas about company leadership and direction as being out of alignment with what was happening in the real world. I found myself struggling against his limiting attitude, but as a leader of a technology company at a time when tech was booming, I opted to remain committed to building the company.

TOUR DE SALESFORCE

A couple of years earlier, sometime around 2000, 2001, I had sold our company's solution to client Steve Cakebread, the CFO at Autodesk and a colleague from our earlier days at Silicon Graphics. Unfortunately, the software didn't meet Autodesk's needs and it left a bad taste in Steve's mouth. Since that incident, however, improvements had been made to the solution, and Steve had moved on from Autodesk to become the CFO of salesforce.com. It was now December 2004, and I thought I'd try to impress the interim CEO by bringing salesforce.com on as a new client.

After working on the proposal for a long time, I arranged to drive up to the salesforce.com office in San Francisco to talk to Steve about it. I thought the moment had come to be bold. But what happened next surprised me.

"It's time, Steve. You need to become a customer," I said, point-blank.

Steve paused, leaned in close, and confided, "Chris, I'm never going to buy this software from you."

Shocked by his quick and flat refusal, I blurted, "Why not?"

He told me he thought the technology was archaic. "It's on-prem. It goes against our religion, everything we believe in." (Even then he knew the cloud was the future, and he had no interest in the old paradigm.)

"But," he added, "you should start your own SaaS company. Do that, and I'll be your first customer!"

CITIZEN GAIN

If I had been smart and taken Steve's advice, this story would be quite different. But being a good corporate citizen, I drove straight back to my office, excited about Steve's feedback and eager to report the news to the interim CEO.

"I didn't get the account," I told him, "but I think this is a wake-up call for us. Let's create a division to handle this as a new product—a SaaS product." I knew that if we didn't disrupt our own business model and go for the software as a service product, someone else would. As you might suspect, my idea wasn't well received. To put it bluntly, the interim CEO thought I was insane.

To be fair, salesforce.com was a pretty new company at the time. Of course, Steve Cakebread had already made a name for himself, and there was his obvious connection to his family's winery. Still, salesforce.com had recently gone public, and what I was proposing would have meant a huge paradigm shift for our board (which, as you've seen from their choice for interim CEO, was a group steeped in tradition and deeply invested in current business practices). They saw no reason to listen to me, a guy with unbridled enthusiasm for what they saw as a crazy idea: *"Scrap everything! The future is in the cloud!"*

A few weeks after that conversation, the CEO called me into his office. Citing creative differences, he fired me. I was given a severance check and asked to walk away quietly.

"It's time for you to go; we don't like your ideas," he said. "SaaS is a fad."

At the time, I was floored. After all, my team had built this organization, and I couldn't imagine it lasting a day without me. I said as much to the chairman of the board, whom I met with after being dismissed by the CEO, in the hope of getting *him* to see the situation my way.

"Son," the chairman said, leaning back in his chair, "let me tell you a story about a bucket of water. Let's say you put your feet in this bucket of water. What happens when you take them out? The water immediately fills the space where your feet were."

In other words, I was completely replaceable.

As I listened to this man's inappropriate, insensitive words, I felt uncomfortable, then angry and resentful. Soon, though, those emotions, coupled with the fact that I knew I had a great idea, caused me to remember Steve's inspiring words. Before I knew it, I was feeling motivated to try something new.

THE YIN AND YANG OF MOTIVATION

In hindsight, I believe getting fired from that company was the best thing that ever happened to me. I realized quickly that I could turn an incredibly negative experience into a positive one; in other words, that disappointment can be motivating. The truth was, when I was told my idea was simply a "fad," it inspired me. I really wanted to prove wrong those who doubted me. I was excited to change the traditional game of business and infuse motivation into a corporate culture that was desperately in need of morale. I was incented to "game the plan," and game it on a high level. I would take advantage of ignored business opportunities and walk away the winner.

Many companies fail when they simply try to be better at the status quo. They follow strategies that have worked in the past, neglecting to take into account constantly shifting and evolving industries—particularly when it comes to technology. I knew I didn't want to do that. I wanted to create a company capable of leading the charge to fully harness the visionary power of the best leaders, and to encourage every individual to dig deep into their unique creative potential. I knew that, given the right goals and incentives, such a culture would combine with motivation to produce the equivalent of rocket fuel.

And so my dismissal soon after the New Year got my feet moving and prompted me to start the company I had envisioned after talking to Steve Cakebread that fateful day in December 2004. Satish and I founded Xactly based on two equally powerful forms of motivation: *negativity*—the lack of support for my creative thinking at a traditionally minded company; and *inspiration*— support from a smart and savvy friend that paired with my personal vision. If the leaders of the company I had worked for had had the courage to try something new, they would now own the incentive compensation management software space entirely. They had the resources and talent to turn an idea into a reality. What they didn't have, in my opinion, was vision beyond the next few quarters of performance. And that lack of vision, the unwillingness to embrace a new idea from an inspired and devoted employee, spawned a major competitor.

When my former traditional-minded CEO passed on the opportunity to adopt a SaaS solution, he underscored the ability that progressive companies have to break into disruptive, emerging markets in order to leapfrog over the competition. The launch of Xactly and our creation of an innovative SaaS solution opened up the incentive compensation management market beyond merely Fortune 500 companies to businesses of all sizes. Today, we have nearly 700 customers whose teams range in size from dozens into the tens of thousands.

THIS BOOK CAN HELP YOU UNLEASH POTENTIAL THROUGH THE SCIENCE OF MOTIVATION

While it's obvious that rewarding performance can propel a company to higher revenue and more success, many company leaders struggle with *how* to unleash the potential within their sales ranks. They don't know how to accurately and effectively align employee self-interest with organizational interest, and so they spend all their time worrying about employees who are taking advantage of them, and not enough time creating better plans.

Game the Plan starts with a revolutionary, three-pronged approach to creating the right plan for your company. The process is based on a combination of academic, anecdotal, and empirical data. The book then guides you through a self-assessment exercise to help you diagnose and fine-tune your incentive strategy effectiveness.

More than just a checklist, however, the book is your source for delving deeply into the empirical science of motivation. The power to unleash sales potential while creating a win-win situation for your company lies in motivation. (Because it's more critical than ever that you understand what truly motivates each of your employees, what you're doing now that doesn't work, and what you can do better, I've devoted an entire chapter—"The Dark Art of Motivation"—to the science of motivation.)

I also examine the software that has been (and is being) developed to support this science, which is quickly gaining ground as *the* way to galvanize employees toward stronger results. *Game the Plan* shares insights for releasing even bigger results, all based on several terabytes of proprietary information gleaned from industry leaders' best practices.

Incentive compensation used to refer strictly to financial bonuses paid to salespeople. Today it includes various non-monetary incentives and spans a variety of workforces, from janitors to bank tellers, truck drivers to CFOs. For the first time ever, companies can intelligently harness the unique motivational composition of their personnel and systematically spike company-wide collaboration and profitability—across every job function and department.

This book will help you stop *fighting* the gamers and start *embracing* them instead. When you've finished reading it, you'll have the tools you need to build win-win incentive plans, knowing—and even relishing—that your employees will find every possible way to earn their checks, bonuses, badges, extra paid time off, or any other incentives you might dangle in front of them.

Your incentive compensation strategy is not a guessing game, nor should your decisions be based on a gut feeling. This book is the map you need to drive your employees to the right behavior with a dialed-in incentive plan.

Incent right. Game on.

CHAPTER 1

ALL THE WORLD'S A STAGE ...
FOR INCENTIVES

The word *incentive* comes from the Latin word *incantare*, which means "to chant or charm." But while the Romans may be credited with the origin of the word, they didn't fare as well with the concept. One factor contributing to the decline of the Roman economy was that the government provided absolutely no incentive to farmers to ramp up production of staple crops. In fact, governors taxed them for increased production instead of rewarding them.[1]

We've come a long way since the days of Julius Caesar. Governments, educational institutions, and businesses (and just about every other type of organization) have used incentives for hundreds— maybe thousands—of years. They've changed with the times, growing more sophisticated and being studied by management science specialists, psychologists, and leaders in government, education, and business. Today, acceptance that incentives are what makes the world go round has resulted in an industry exclusively designed to help organizations motivate employees to increase productivity and, ultimately, profit.

The way we incent will continue to evolve in response to changes in the world. But what hasn't changed—what won't change—is what incentives are at their very core: tactics we use when we want to bring about change and steer people's actions in specific directions.

The *Oxford American Dictionary* Webster's defines incentive as "a thing that motivates or encourages one to do something; a payment or concession to stimulate greater output or investment." It's also worth noting that, according to Webster's, the first known use of the word *incentivize* was in 1970 coined in the late 1960s.

At its very best, an incentive is also a trade. In order for an incentive to fulfill its purpose, *both* parties must gain from the action the incented person makes.

Let's consider what these win-win situations have looked like over the past few centuries.

PIRATES OF THE COMPENSATION

For all we know, the use of incentives may have started with the Cro-Magnons, but since we have yet to find evidence on cave walls, let's start in the golden age of piracy, between 1716 and 1722.

When you think of early-eighteenth-century pirates, you probably think of illegal activity, unruly mayhem, and violence. Your perceptions are no doubt correct. But as disorderly as a band of pirates may have seemed on the surface, it was no accident that they ruled the seas. It boiled down to manpower. The average crew size of a pirate ship was between 80 and 120 men. Captain Henry Morgan, who led the largest pirate organization of the time, commanded two thousand men and thirty-seven ships. Yet a typical merchant ship had fewer than twenty crewmen aboard.[2] What gave Captain Morgan and his fellow pirate captains the ability to attract so many more men than anyone else? A winning approach.

When you think of the words *pirate captain*, swashbuckling adventures probably come to mind. But you might be selling men like Captain Morgan short by not seeing them as leaders who had developed a management structure highly focused on engaging, motivating, and retaining their "employees." To better understand how incentives worked on the high seas, let's spend a day in the life of the highly effective Captain Morgan.

Recruitment, Engagement, Motivation—Pirate Style

His dress code was undoubtedly more relaxed on the ships he commanded, but Captain Morgan decidedly had a lot in common with today's CEOs. His goal was simple: to get as much "booty" as possible by terrorizing the Spaniards more efficiently than his competitors did.

Like the average CEO, Captain Morgan experienced pain points.

First, he had to recruit and retain the manpower necessary for successful plunder. This meant competing with merchant ships and the Royal Navy for the best men.

Second, he had to motivate the crew to be as productive as possible while incenting them not to steal booty—a pretty tall order when you consider the lack of ethics and morals among these bad boys. But the captain could not do so with an iron fist or in any way that was contrary to the crew's goals. Otherwise, he would be walking the plank.

Lucky for Captain Morgan, recruitment was made easy in large part because of the "leadership" exercised by the captains of the merchant ships, men driven by a solitary goal: to make the absentee owners of the ships happy. Quite often this came at the cost of the happiness of crew members, who were frequently cheated and treated cruelly. These sea dogs didn't need much convincing to jump ship.[3]

With crews in place, Captain Morgan and others of his ilk made sure their jack-tars toed the line by incenting them to adhere to a strict code of behavior. While important positions such as captain, quartermaster, and surgeon received a bit more of the bounty, for the most part the loot was divided evenly among the crew. A motto of "no prey, no pay" motivated all pirates to put forth their best efforts. Those who attempted to steal bounty were swiftly and severely punished. But such instances were rare because the men knew that if they performed, the captain was a man of his word who would give them their fair share of the loot. The pirates were less likely to pinch it and more likely to work as a team.[4]

Savvy Captain Morgan also knew the best incentive involves a payment or concession to stimulate greater output or investment. Merchant seamen in the period between 1689 and 1740 earned thirteen to thirty-three British pounds per year. In comparison, a pirate who had a good day on the water that ended with the capture of a treasure-laden fleet could earn one thousand pounds.[5]

Doing the math, that means it would take the lowest-paid seaman seventy-seven years to earn what a pirate could earn in one day!

How's that for sufficiently motivating your team to steal, murder, and risk death (if caught)?

Captain Morgan and his men were bad, but they left a legacy when it comes to the understanding and use of incentives. After all, how many CEOs do you know who have a popular brand of rum named after them?

THE NAPOLEONIC WARS: WINNING BATTLES WITH INCENTIVES

Let's hop to the late 1700s and early 1800s, a time when incentives proved their mettle on the battlefield.

Napoleon Bonaparte, tyrant though he may have been, perfected the use of incentives during his reign as emperor of France, turning a legion of ragtag soldiers into a highly motivated group of conquerors. Standing only five feet two inches and teased as a child for being the boy from Corsica who couldn't speak proper French, Napoleon had something to prove. Like many generals before him, he used fear to motivate. When Major-General Louis Berthier met Napoleon in 1796, he said, "I don't know why, but the little bastard scares me."[6]

Tight Budget? Create Creative Incentives

But fear alone wouldn't fix the mess Napoleon stepped into. When the brilliant military strategist first met his army, the men were in ill health and hadn't been paid in months. The soldiers knew the country was broke and that payment was unlikely, regardless of their behavior, so there was no incentive for them to perform.

Knowing that his success was tied to the soldiers around him, and that *their* success depended on their level of enthusiasm for their missions, Napoleon's goal was to create a win-win situation for himself, his soldiers, and, ultimately, his country. But like many of today's CEOs who face budget cuts and constraints, Napoleon had little to work with. If he was going to win wars, he was going to have to think outside the box.

Therefore, he stood in front of his men, and made them this promise:

> Soldiers, you are naked, ill fed! The Government owes you much; it can give you nothing. Your patience, the courage you display in the midst of these rocks, are admirable; but they procure you no glory, no fame is reflected on you. I seek to lead you into the most fertile plains in the world. Rich provinces, great cities will be in your power. There, you will find honor, glory, riches.[7]

Piedmont, the Precursor to Profit Sharing

Napoleon understood that appreciating his soldiers was one way to gain their loyalty. He also knew of no better way to show appreciation to an unpaid army than through monetary rewards. So when his soldiers performed well in Italy's Piedmont region, causing the enemy army to surrender, Napoleon demanded the vanquished foe's silver and gold.[8]

Napoleon used that silver and gold to pay his men, establishing the link between pay and performance. From that point forward, his men knew that, regardless of the financial state of France, if they battled hard enough and won they would be rewarded with wartime spoils. Just as modern profit-sharing plans motivate collaborative success, this was enough of an incentive for these starving, ragged men to change their behavior.

Appreciation, Recognition, and "Gamification"

Since money was tight, and tangible rewards not always accessible, Napoleon had to think of other forms of motivation. One way he showed his appreciation for soldiers was by creating the Legion of Honour, which recognized individual men for their contributions.[9] And in what might be one of the earliest forms of "gamification,"

Napoleon rewarded men who were named by their battalion leaders as "bravest," "strongest," or any other number of superlatives by giving them medals from his own jacket. You can bet that small but meaningful incentive kept soldiers on their toes and wanting to perform their best.

Despite significant odds, Napoleon's army went on to capture much of Europe before being defeated at Leipzig and Waterloo, proving that even in tough times, a thoughtful approach to incentives yields win-win results.

THE 1920s: A DECADE OF PLENTY AND THE BIRTH OF THE AMERICAN SALESMAN

In the 1920s, great economic and social transformation gave birth to modern sales management.

Formally Introducing . . . The Sales Incentive

The Roaring Twenties was a period marked by major advances in technology and manufacturing that led to innovation in business, changing social roles, and economic prosperity. These advancements improved the agricultural sector, promoted growth in the automobile industry, provided electricity to homes and businesses, improved communication with the development of radio networks and long-distance telephone ability, and made life at home easier with the invention of time-saving household appliances.[10]

Improved manufacturing processes and the introduction of the assembly line resulted in the faster and cheaper production of automobiles, making them more accessible to the masses. For example, by 1928, a Model T Ford rolled off the production line every twenty seconds and cost the average American worker about three months' wages—instead of the pre–World War I price of two years' wages.[11]

As business machines, appliances, and cars were manufactured on scales never seen before, organizations needed to find new ways to create demand for and compete in selling them. And so they hired droves of salesmen. But these weren't the peddlers and snake oil salesmen of yesteryear who sold elixirs, cure-alls, and tonics they vowed would do everything from grow hair to bring God to heathens.[12] Manufacturing had created a system for producing goods, and it was time for organizations to approach sales in the same systematic way.

Giants such as Eastman-Kodak, Coca-Cola, General Electric, and Wrigley's assigned territories, set quotas, and began to measure success. Salespeople were being asked to do more than ever before: explain products, and create demand for products, even service products.[13]

At IBM, Chief Executive Thomas J. Watson Sr. hired only the best and the brightest from the country's most prestigious universities. He developed a six-week training period to guarantee that they knew the product and could sell it in an educated manner. Watson put his salesmen in conservative suits, taught them how to conduct themselves among professionals, and coached them about pushing customers to buy products they might not otherwise buy.[14]

Burgeoning capitalism was surely strengthening the link between pay and performance, which expanded well beyond the sales office and into general society. In 1930, Babe Ruth made $80,000. When he was asked why he should make $5,000 more than President Hoover, he responded, "I'm having a better year than he is."[16]

Large companies invested a lot in "professionalizing" their employees, and productivity was critical to their success. To hedge their bets, corporate leaders began to focus on sales incentives. For the most part, these leaders used simple cash incentives coupled with recognition. IBM's Chief Executive Watson, for example, developed a scheme that rewarded salespeople who met their quota with bonuses and induction into the elite Hundred Percent Club.[15]

Eventually, a tanking economy and an imbalance between labor supply and demand shelved incentive-based compensation during the Great Depression. But it was far from dead.

DELAYED GRATIFICATION? A REVIEW OF INCENTIVES IN THE 1940s

In the 1940s, organizations moved beyond the idea that incentives could drive behavior in general, such as putting forth best effort, and focused instead on how they could be used to drive specific behaviors, like selling a certain number of units within a specific time period. During this decade (and actually up through the 1960s), the use of incentives took on a new level of creativity. Allow me to set the stage for that shift by rolling the clock back to the early twentieth century.

Short-Term Incentives, Long-Term Lags

Moguls in the early 1900s, including Andrew Carnegie and John D. Rockefeller, were set on building companies that would last forever and sustain their families through steady growth. That tack was an incentive for leaders, who were often relatives, to think long term. But as more and more non-family-run businesses entered the marketplace, the professional managers who led these organizations were less concerned about future success and more concerned about success while they were on board. It wasn't uncommon for such managers to focus only on the upcoming year, or even the upcoming quarter.

In a competitive environment that equated success with sustained growth, short-term bonuses weren't driving the behavior needed to meet long-term goals.

Pay for Performance, Long-Term Style

Organizations introduced long-term bonuses as early as the 1940s.[17] These incentives shifted away from the large "gift" bonuses of the 1920s that were piled on top of high salaries. Rather, the new bonus structure paid out bonuses in three to five years, and only when specific long-term goals, such as increased revenue, were realized. These incentives were designed to help employees see beyond immediate gratification and instead make decisions that would affect the long-term health and prosperity of the company.

Although long-term bonuses debuted in the decade following the Great Depression, their impact wasn't really felt until the 1960s, when they represented a greater share of an employee's compensation package. Typically, long-term incentives were connected to a company's profits and were paid in cash or in stock over a certain number of years.[18] Stock options became a popular addition to the long-term incentive mix especially in the 1950s, when tax reform legislation that drove up income tax rates made stock options an attractive, and less taxable, alternative.

This tax reform caused organizations to get increasingly creative when it came to incentives. While cash was king prior to tax reform, and was viewed as the most dependable way of getting—and keeping—productive bodies in office chairs, big tax hits reduced the effect of this dangling carrot. How could organizations motivate their employees in spite of tax reform? Once again, they responded to changes in the world by changing the way they incented. Enter perquisites.

PERKS—COMPENSATION'S CAFFEINE JOLT IN THE 1950s

Perquisites, commonly known today as "perks," were introduced to compensation plans in the 1950s. Because of the tax situation described in the previous section, organizations needed to find a way to motivate employees that didn't involve money, and perks were particularly ingenious because they tapped into a significant human need—the hunger for recognition.

Recognition as Reward

It was probably no coincidence that perks entered the compensation scene about the same time that psychologist Abraham Maslow introduced his "Hierarchy of Needs," which turned out to be the foundation for many recognition and motivation theories. Maslow believed that every individual operates according to a motivational system composed of five hierarchal needs, which he organized into a pyramid. Basic needs such as food, water, and sleep provide the foundation of the pyramid, followed by safety needs, such as health, family, and jobs. Social needs, met by things like love, family, and belonging, sit on top of safety needs.[19]

Toward the top of the pyramid, right before the individual reaches self-actualization, are esteem needs. According to Maslow, all people have a need for self-respect and self-esteem, which they reach through achievement, status, responsibility, and reputation.[20] And in the 1950s particularly, nothing said you had "arrived" more than the tangibles others could see and envy—a big corner office or a Cadillac Coupe de Ville.

Perks are defined as any type of special right or privilege enjoyed as a result of one's position. Perks in the Fabulous Fifties ranged from lavish to practical, from country club memberships, company cars, and use of vacation homes owned by the organization to personalized parking spaces and private secretaries. During this decade, perks typically came with the job title; employees were thus incented to achieve and achieve, and then achieve some more, to quickly climb the corporate ladder.

The movie *Will Success Spoil Rock Hunter?*, which was released in 1957 and starred Tony Randall and Jayne Mansfield, provides great insight—albeit with satirical potshots—into the importance of being recognized and the motivating powers of perks during the 1950s.

A funny precursor to today's *Mad Men*, the movie portrays the eponymous protagonist as a struggling, low-ranking ad man who longs to succeed. Why? Rock Hunter's ultimate goal is not more money, a bigger house, or a fancier car. What he really wants is the key to the company's executive washroom. What follows is a series of events (and several hilarious lines that surprisingly escaped censorship) showing that Rock Hunter is willing to go to great lengths, even jeopardize love, just to get his hands on this tangible status symbol.

Today's Perks—Not Your Grandfather's Favorites

Those mid-twentieth-century perks became ever more extravagant as we entered the 1990s and the first decade of the twenty-first century. The media loves to attack perks, because when they're perceived as being abused, they make a good story. For instance, recent public outrage resulted in new Securities and Exchange Commission disclosure rules, which now call for detailed disclosure of any perquisite in excess of $10,000. But did that put the kibosh on country clubs? Did executive jet flight plans get jettisoned? The answer is a surprising no. According to data released after a review of 2012 proxy statements, reductions in executive perks markedly slowed, and some organizations even added what they considered to be justifiable perks.[21]

Detractors of perks argue that because they aren't strongly linked to performance, they do nothing to motivate employees. But studies such as one conducted by Raghuram Rajan of the International Monetary Fund and Julie Wulf of the University of Pennsylvania's Wharton School show that perks do, indeed, boost production and have a good effect on the company overall.[22]

According to Ask.com's 2012 "State of the Workplace: Benefits and Perks" study, 95% of Americans consider job benefits and perks before deciding whether to remain at their current job or to accept a new one.[23]

Today's perks, unlike those offered in the 1950s, are no longer ego-driven tools used only for executives. Many organizations have applied what we know about motivation and recognition to developing more modern perks for the entire workforce, designed to attract, retain, and provide an overall sense of well-being to specific groups of individuals based on what is important to them. While media coverage has made *perks* a dirty word, more often than not perks are used for the mutual benefit of both the employee and the organization, without having a negative impact on the investor.

Perks of yore may have fallen out of fashion, along with double-pleated trousers and skinny ties, but as a general concept they've remained. Just as individual needs and desires change over the years, so, too, will the way companies offer this flexible incentive.

EVERYBODY LOVES AN IPO

As I mentioned in the earlier section called "Pay for Performance, Long-Term Style," the stock option as an incentive was first introduced in the 1950s, when tax reform made cash bonuses unpalatable, but was perfected in the 1990s, when cash-strapped technology

PROGRESSIVE PERKS

Consider just a few of the ways today's more evolved perks are being used to develop win-win situations:

- Google taps into its employees' desire for health and an improved quality of life by offering free food at lunch and dinner, massages and yoga, backup child-care assistance, and $12,000 annually in tuition reimbursement.[24]

- InDemand Interpreting, a company that connects patients and health care providers with interpreters via video, taps into its employees' desire for recognition and trust by awarding high-performing employees with a "box lunch"—the keys to CEO Daniel Pirestani's Porsche Boxter to drive to a restaurant for a leisurely company-paid lunch.[25]

- Netflix taps into its employees' desire for freedom and autonomy by focusing on what employees do for the company, not on how many days they work. Translation: unlimited vacation time.[26]

- LoadSpring Solutions, an enterprise software company, taps into its employees' desire for growth and experience by offering employees who travel abroad up to $5,000 and an extra week so they can spend some time expanding their horizons when they are finished with their business obligations.[27]

- Patagonia, the outdoor apparel manufacturer, taps into its employees' desire to make the world a better place by giving employees two weeks of full-paid leave each year to work for a green nonprofit of their choice.[28]

and dot-com businesses made stock options the long-term incentive plans of choice. By 2002, about ten million Americans were receiving stock options as part of their compensation plans.[29]

No Money? No Problem. Attracting Top Talent at Rock-Bottom Prices

Organizations jumped on the stock option bandwagon for several reasons. First, in an effort to curb excessive executive salaries, Congress imposed tax penalties on all base salaries over $1 million. Second, "invisible" stock options weren't really expenses, so they didn't affect any organization's bottom line. They were a terrific way to attract top talent without a cash investment, and because of their vesting periods, they ensured that employees stuck around for a while. Third, these stock options had a built-in, foolproof incentive. Because the employees' eventual payout was tied to the organization's success, conventional wisdom said they would do their damnedest to make sure the company was a success.

Employees loved stock options because visions of highly desired initial public offerings (IPOs) danced in their heads. If you were an employee who was offered stock options as part of your compensation plan in the 1990s, you prayed for an IPO à la Whole Foods, Starbucks, Yahoo, Amazon.com, or eBay—all companies whose market caps grew at astounding rates. When Google went public in 2004, for instance, it turned one thousand employees into millionaires almost overnight. Five years later there were even more millionaires, and even a few billionaires, as a result of that IPO.[30]

But Are Stock Options All They're Cracked Up to Be?

In 2010, a study done by the National Center for Employee Ownership (NCEO) estimated that about nine million American employees held stock options, down about 30 percent from 2001. NCEO blames the decline on changes in accounting rules as well as on increased shareholder pressure to reduce the dilution of existing shares.[31]

It's true that the number of stock options being offered has declined, but it's not because everyone doesn't love an IPO. Companies are still using IPOs to incent and motivate, but they are being much more thoughtful about how they do so.

As it turned out, the stock options as offered in the 1990s didn't have as much of a long-term influence as leadership initially thought. Employees were gaining more when stock prices rose quarter to quarter, which caused them to focus more on short-term goals than on long-term goals. Stock options are still a great way to incent employees, but only when they are *part* of an organization's long-term incentive plan, not the whole plan. Many of today's companies use stock options to influence company camaraderie and collaboration, but they combine them with performance shares and restricted stock.

=====

If the history of compensation has taught us anything it's that we're on the right track with incentive compensation. But until recently, we've had no real, quantifiable way to measure retention, engagement, and productivity. In the next chapter, we'll explore new technologies and see how they can be used to reveal exactly what organizations must do to incent their teams right.

Visit www.GameThePlan.com to watch videos that share how to apply this chapter's principles in your own company.

CHAPTER 2

THE PERFECT TECHNOLOGY STORM: INCENTING A DATA-DRIVEN (AND DATA-DEPENDENT!) SOCIETY

History has taught us that incentives matter. In the last chapter, I offered some famous and not-so-famous examples of how incentives have been used to change behavior both within and outside of the workplace. Incentives influence more than just sales teams; they impact every area of our lives.

Consider, for example, how the price of gas affects behavior. When gas prices reached new highs in the 1970s, people made a real effort to consolidate trips and to carpool. Automobile manufacturers introduced more fuel-efficient cars, such as the Honda Civic. When gas was comparable in price to bottled water in the 1980s and 1990s, gas-guzzling SUVs came into fashion. With gas prices again at record highs today, more fuel-efficient cars, such as the Toyota Prius, other hybrids, and electric vehicles like the

Tesla Model S are in great demand. According to an article by Bill Howard published in the May 15, 2013, edition of *Extreme Tech*, Tesla had U.S. sales of approximately 4,750 cars in the first quarter of 2013.[1] The high first quarter numbers were likely due to the fact that Tesla had disrupted the industry with the only electric sports car on the market.

As an interesting aside, during a keynote discussion at the 2013 D11 Conference, Tesla Motors cofounder, CEO, and product architect Elon Musk admitted that getting into the electric car business was perceived as stupid, insane, or both. But he said he did it anyway when it was clear that other automobile manufacturers weren't going to enter the space.[2] How's that for an incentive?

Economists and researchers have published thousands of studies suggesting that the human reaction to incentives may be instinctive, and that incentives are deeply significant. In fact, while researching for this book, I couldn't find a single study to the contrary. Savvy organizations recognize the importance of incentives across all areas, and as a result they are developing carefully considered incentive compensation plans for their teams.

In chapter one I pointed out the ways in which the economy, culture, and various trends have influenced the way organizations incented their people throughout history. Now let's look more closely at the situation we're in today and how it is affecting the ways we incent.

AHEM. HELLO? IT'S INCENTIVES! I'M BACK, REMEMBER ME?

In 2008, hot on the heels of the 2001 recession, which many economists believe to be the worst financial crisis since the Great Depression hit, the world's strongest financial institutions threatened to collapse, and stock markets all over the world plummeted. Governments scrambled to rescue banks. Americans couldn't turn on their televisions or open the newspaper without seeing stories about evictions and foreclosures, housing bubbles bursting, and once-robust businesses closing their doors for good. During this time, failing businesses, desperate to save their skins, began downsizing.

On November 7, 2008, the *New York Times* published an article by Peter S. Goodman in its Economy section. Goodman noted that the unemployment rate, which had spiked to 6.5 percent one month earlier, was at its highest in fourteen years. In October alone, the economy had lost another 240,000 jobs, upping the total number of jobs lost since the beginning of the year to 1.2 million.[3]

But the worst was yet to come.

By March 2010, even as the U.S. economy was beginning to emerge from the recession, the unemployment rate skyrocketed to 9.9 percent. According to the U.S. Bureau of Labor Statistics, there were fifteen million unemployed Americans that month. That number didn't even include unemployed part-time workers, job seekers who had been out of work for so long they had basically given up on their search, and those who fell through the statistical cracks because they no longer qualified for unemployment.

You can probably guess where I'm going here: If you were employed during this time, you felt lucky to have a job. Damn lucky. As a matter of fact, just *having* a job, and continuing to avoid the chopping block, was incentive enough for you to perform. In fact, according to a July 2010 Center for Creative Leadership report called "Employee Engagement: Has It Been a Bull Market?," as layoffs increased throughout the workforce, employees became more engaged.[4] One result of this increase in employee engagement was that companies put incentives on the back burner. To hang tight to their profits they cut bonus and commission

programs, and they reduced benefits. They also put the kibosh
on perks. They weren't worried about their sales reps leaving for
greener pastures because—let's be real—*there weren't any greener
pastures they could go to!*

For many managers and leaders, minimizing incentives seemed
a good way to stay afloat in rough waters. But have organizations
ignored incentives for too long?

Research indicates that they have.

In a survey of nine hundred American workers conducted by
Right Management in 2009, 60 percent said they would leave their
current employers in 2010 as the economy improved. As the job
market continues to improve, organizations that want to retain
their rock star reps now need to start looking at ways to reengage
them and incent them to stick around.[5]

With the unemployment rate at 7.6 percent as of May 2013,
employees hardly have the upper hand. But as the economy
improves, it's very likely that high-performing employees will be
the first to walk out the door as better opportunities arise. Organizations that remain complacent—those that don't dig deep
and focus on how to inspire and influence their post recession
employees—will feel the hurt as turnover increases. Unless . . .

WHAT'S GOOD FOR BETTY ISN'T GOOD FOR BRITTNEY: MANAGING AND MOTIVATING THE MULTIGENERATIONAL WORKFORCE

At a time when organizations need to refocus on how they motivate and pay employees, they have the additional task of creating
incentive plans that speak to the needs of more than one group—
four groups, to be exact. For the first time in history, four generations are working together in most workplaces: Traditionalists,
Baby Boomers, Gen X, and Gen Y.

- **Traditionalists.** Born between 1920 and 1945, Traditionalists are non-risk-takers who are interested in planning for the future. They value the team approach and are driven by formal, public recognition. In a 2010 survey of three hundred employees conducted by AchieveGlobal, Traditionalists resorted to "feeling good about what I do" when asked about the most important goal of their job.[6] They aren't in the habit of spending on themselves, so non-cash incentives speak loudly. The Traditionalists within your organization might be motivated by seeing their names displayed on a public leaderboard, by being featured in the company newsletter, or by receiving plaques or other tangibles in public ceremonies.

- **Baby Boomers.** Born between 1946 and 1964, Baby Boomers matured during an age of economic prosperity and are extremely competitive and willing to work hard for their rewards. They prefer long-term employment to short-term employment, and they also like being formally recognized for their achievements. Otherwise known as the "Me" generation, Boomers appreciate job security and good pay and want to see a direct link between accomplishments and rewards. This generation enjoys being spoiled; hence, personalized pats on the back go a long way toward making them feel appreciated. Many of Nordstrom's sales associates are from this generation, and consequently, the company developed its Pacesetter award (for top-selling employees) with the needs and desires of Boomers in mind. Those who earn Pacesetter status are eligible for cash awards, a higher merchandise discount than non-Pacesetters, Nordstrom stock, and public recognition. The longer a salesperson is a Pacesetter, the more awards she can earn.[7]

- **Gen X**. Born between 1965 and 1980, the Gen X (or "Slacker") generation is entrepreneurial, technologically savvy, creative, and independent. Because Gen Xers have worked through many difficult economies, they don't believe in job security or expect to work for the same organization for an extended period of time, making them a difficult group to retain. Gen Xers value family over work, aren't willing to work long hours, and are motivated by situations that improve work-life balance. They want a workplace environment that is challenging, and they find meaning in learning new things. Intel may have had Generation X in mind when they came up with their sabbatical program. The semiconductor chip company incents its employees to stick around for the long haul by rewarding them with two months off—on the house, with full paychecks and benefits—for every seven years on the payroll.[8] This incentive to remain with Intel gives the independent, work-life-balance-loving, knowledge-seeking Gen Xer plenty of time to pursue hobbies and interests outside of work, hang with family or friends, or take a class.

- **Gen Y**. Born after 1981, Gen Yers, also known as "Millennials" or the "Trophy" generation, are optimistic, highly confident, results-driven employees who value people over companies. They want it all—money, flexibility, work-life balance, recognition, praise, promotion—and they want it *now*. Like the generations before them, they seek meaningful work, but they aren't willing to climb the ladder to get it. They want their work to matter to them from day one. It's easy to dismiss Gen Yers as spoiled brats, but companies that do so miss out on their optimism, technological savvy, and entrepreneurial approach to work.

Companies that recognize this generation as the future of the workforce are developing specific incentives designed to give Millennials what they want while getting the most out of them. For example, in addition to offering money, some organizations have begun to reward Generation Y with more vacation time and work-from-home privileges when they meet their goals.

INCENTIVE OR REWARDS PROGRAM?
WHAT'S THE DIFFERENCE?

Amid this discussion about how to motivate the four generations within most American workplaces, it's important to distinguish between incentives and rewards. An incentive program motivates a sales representative to reach certain goals; a rewards program thanks him or her for a job well done.

If a bonus shows up in a rep's March 15 paycheck for products he sold in February, that's an incentive program. If that same rep receives a flat bonus at the end of the year, that's a rewards program.

Use this surefire way to determine whether you've created an incentive program or a rewards program at your shop: If it takes you two or more months to measure and compensate for a specific goal, you've created a rewards program, not an incentive one

Determining how to use incentives to motivate sales reps has always been on the top of management's list, and it's always been a difficult task. Today's complex workforce demographics make this job even harder. On the one hand, leaders need to know what each of these groups has in common and then come up with plans that reward collaborative behavior. On the other hand, they need to incent and reward the unique abilities and skills that each group brings to the table, and that means knowing *exactly* what makes each group tick before devising an incentive compensation strategy designed to attract, retain, and engage top performers from each of the four specific groups.

THE 411 ON MOTIVATING MILLENNIALS

Gen Y is taking over the workforce. These Millennials are known for being:

- Self-confident
- Ambitious and motivated to succeed
- Digitally savvy and socially connected
- Hardwired for instant gratification

A demographic that demands recognition for work well done, Millennials aren't motivated by paychecks alone. In addition to monetary incentives and perks, they want accolades when they meet their marks. So, appreciate away—with words, recognition in team and all staff meetings, and even with plaques and trophies. More than any other generation, Millennials are more likely to move on if a job doesn't meet their material *and* psychological expectations; retaining them means engaging and rewarding them for jobs well done. Coaching and mentoring is important to Gen Yers, who have been guided through life by parents and teachers.

To motivate Millennials:

- Define job roles clearly
- Recognize individual performance
- Reward desired behaviors
- Provide tangible, incremental steps up the career ladder
- Provide consistent feedback, coaching, and mentoring to keep them on track

WHAT CAROL AND COURTNEY HAVE IN COMMON: IDENTIFYING SHARED VALUES

While there are plenty of differences among employees from these four generations, studies show they also have much in common. Jennifer Deal, a research scientist with the Center for Creative Leadership and the author of *Retiring the Generation Gap: How Employees Young and Old Can Find Common Ground*, spoke with more than three thousand corporate leaders to find out what members of each group value. She discovered that Traditionalists, Baby Boomers, Gen X, and Gen Y alike value respect, trust, opportunity, and family.[9]

When it comes to incenting your multigenerational sales force, identifying the values shared by an entire workforce despite age and cultural influences is key. Just remember, however, it's equally important to realize that each generation might have a different way of *defining* those values.

For example, although each generation values "opportunity," Traditionalists may view opportunity as additional ways that allow them to contribute to their retirement funds, while Gen Yers may see opportunity as anything that allows them to better align their jobs with their passions.

When you consider the differences in how people define respect, trust, opportunity, and family, you can then develop incentive compensation procedures and strategies to drive the desired behaviors of each generation.

Notice I am *not* suggesting that you design different goals for each generation. Though each group is looking for something different and is motivated by unique drivers, all should be working toward your organization's common goals. So find out what motivates different groups of employees to meet objectives, and incent accordingly.

Let's look at an example of how this plays out in a large business whose goal is to improve quality. Traditionalists might be motivated to meet or exceed quota by a public ceremony in which they receive a material reward; Baby Boomers might be motivated to improve customer service grades by a cash bonus or additional office perks; and Gen Xers might be motivated to increase short-term sales of a specific product when promised rewards that align with their desire for work-life balance, such as additional time off or flextime. You can really have fun with those highly social Gen Yers: Promise them a Ping-Pong table in the staff room or the newest electronic device and you'll most likely see their individual goals met faster than Apple updates its operating systems! (For examples of companies that are creating highly unique incentives for different groups of employees, see the sidebar titled "Progressive Perks" in chapter one.)

Understanding what drives your workforce will also help you design unique benefits and perk plans, ensuring that you have meaningful options for each group. But do you have the information you need to determine what your unique workforce appreciates, needs, and responds to? Perhaps you've tapped into some data, but there's so much more available for the taking—*massive* amounts of it, in fact.

BIG DATA GOES MAINSTREAM

Major advancements in technology have turned us into a data-driven (and data-dependent!) society. We're bombarded with data in our everyday lives, and we use it to make such important decisions as what college to attend and where to live in retirement. We also use it for mundane reasons. Can't figure out what to make for dinner? All you need to do is type #whatsfordinner into your Twitter search bar to find hundreds of delicious recipes. Want to know Macklemore's real name? Just google your question to find the answer. Even the average twelve-year-old—who updates his or her status on Facebook regularly, "tweets" on Twitter ten times a day, and loads photos to Instagram with amazing speed—is contributing to the creation of data.

Using technology to access information has become so mainstream that major dictionaries list "Google" as a verb.

The constant stream of easily accessible information, combined with the pool of knowledge that is the Internet, has certainly changed the way we live and think.

It's also changed the way we work.

According to IBM, the people of the world create 2.5 quintillion bytes of data per day. About 90 percent of the data we consume globally today has been created in the past two years alone.[10] To succeed in business and come up with winning tactics, organizations must sift through much of that data to figure out how their brand is perceived, what their competitors are doing, whether or not their customers are happy, and much, much more. But if you think it's easier to get the answers you need because information is more public today than it's ever been, think again. You can get buried under all that data if you don't have the right strategies for managing and accessing it.

In a report he published on February 6, 2001, Doug Laney of the Meta Group was the first to use the term *big data* to describe data sets that are so huge they're difficult to manage.[11] In that post, he identifies three areas—the three Vs—that make data sets challenging to manage in the workplace:

1. **Velocity:** The speed at which data is created. As the velocity increases, businesses are tasked with finding better ways to keep up with it and manage it.

2. **Variety:** The ever-expanding types of data we encounter. Companies are collecting and storing more types of data to get a better handle on how to meet strategic goals and improve communication with employees, customers, and partners. This greater variety of data, of course, requires new ways of storing and retrieving it.

3. **Volume:** The growth of data, and the massive amounts of information that must be managed and analyzed.

When structuring incentives, you can allow big data to be either a brick or a life buoy. On one hand, there's so much data to consider that it's tempting to hit autopilot and develop one-size-fits-all plans that have worked in the past; the moving target aspect of constantly changing data might make you feel like giving up. On the other hand, your data gives you access to valuable internal and external information—quota attainment, productivity, customer satisfaction, turnover rates, industry changes, pay scales, and territory information—but only if you can find a way to organize it.

In their book titled *Big Data: A Revolution That Will Transform How We Live, Think, and Work,* authors Kenneth Cukier and Viktor Mayer-Schonberger call big data "the raw material of business."[12] But how do you organize these raw materials to give you the answers you need to develop effective incentive compensation plans?

SPREADSHEETS? NAH.

Many organizations use spreadsheet applications to manage their incentive compensation programs because they believe that spreadsheets take human error out of the process of crunching numbers. But that's just not the case. Think of it this way: Would you balance your company's books with an abacus? Probably not. But if you're

GUESSTIMATING COMPENSATION

In 2005, Computer Associates (CA) missed their commissions accrual balance and had to completely restate their earnings.[13] Until that point, the company hadn't based its accruals off the compensation data that came out of its commission system. The traditional compensation tools it was using—namely, spreadsheets—didn't have the sophistication to deliver detailed reports, so CA had been guesstimating commission amounts and coming up with inaccurate numbers.

You can't take 110% of attainment and assume your accruals will also be 110%. Some reps will reach 60% of quota, and some will reach 150%. Depending on your compensation plan, reps who surpass the 100% mark might get a higher bonus rate. So you have to take extra payout into account when you're estimating numbers. And acceleration in a plan is generally much steeper than deceleration, putting companies that are doing well surprisingly at risk of missing earnings.

At CA, every deal it closed resulted in about 110–115 people getting paid. This complicated its efforts at wrangling numbers. To make things even more complex, it was in the process of acquiring a lot of smaller companies, and therefore more reps. CA's practice was to keep incoming reps on their existing plans and let them cover the territories they'd covered for the original company. This created conflict with CA's existing reps, who were already covering some of the same territories. To pacify all parties, CA paid all of the reps.

CA's situation was a perfect storm of circumstances that, ironically, stemmed from its growth and success. As a result of over-acceleration, its global miss was 25%. This could have been avoided had it put an automated compensation management system in place before it started its acquisitions.

still using thirty-year-old spreadsheet technology to track compensation and to drive employee motivation, that's more or less what you are doing. And you're not alone. I work in Silicon Valley, a competitive and progressive region, yet every day I interface with leaders of companies that sell cutting-edge, high-tech products who still somehow justify motivating their teams using outdated, ineffective spreadsheet applications as their primary tool.

Spreadsheets are not infallible, especially as the numbers get larger and the formulas get more complex. What follows is a personal story that underscores my point.

THE $72,000 COMPENSATION MISTAKE

In the mid-1990s—before the Internet, cell phones, and direct deposit were the norm—I was a West Coast sales manager at Silicon Graphics, Inc. (SGI), whose policy was to reward each of the area sales managers with an $8,000 bonus when we met our goals.

After one seemingly average quarter, I was shocked (and thrilled) when a bonus check for $80,000 landed on my desk. I looked around for a hidden camera. Not seeing one, I briefly considered absconding to Tahiti. But that dream was short-lived; I knew in my gut that an accounting mistake had been made. I walked to the other side of the building and handed the check to the compensation administrator. "I think maybe there's been a mistake," I said.

> **She looked at the amount, then back at me in shock. "Do you realize that we would never have caught this?"**

At the time, SGI was paying between seven and eight hundred salespeople tens of millions of dollars per quarter. A $72,000 error was not likely to get caught. In fact, an error triple that amount would have gone unseen, because as the admin soon discovered, two other area managers in competing territories had gotten similarly flawed checks. (They were my friends, and I can't say they were very happy with me!) Because our bonus payouts were calculated from the same spreadsheet, the total error amounted to a whopping $216,000.

Spreadsheet mistakes happen every day, in every company of every size, in all different areas, from paychecks to quota attainment.

So if managing data with spreadsheets isn't the greatest of ideas, as this story illustrates, what better ways do we have of getting a handle on it?

GETTING BIG RETURNS FROM BIG DATA

I like to compare managing big data to the hit cooking show *Chopped*. During each episode of this program, four chefs are each given a basket of random, incongruous foods, access to a pantry full of staples, and a full range of cooking appliances. The task? Make culinary sense of the chaos.

At the beginning of the show, I'm always a bit on edge. With the clock ticking, contestants hurry to prepare the odd mix of ingredients, alternately slicing and dicing and frantically searching pantry shelves for the seasonings that will help pull their dishes together. It's a hectic process initially, but eventually each chef finds the right combination of complementary flavors, and then attractively arranges his or her culinary masterpiece on a plate to be presented to the judges.

The process is much the same for corporations that are tackling big data management: It's hard to know where to begin, or how to make sense of the mess. But just like the chefs on *Chopped*, once management finds, analyzes, and organizes the data, they can dish up an effective incentive compensation strategy.

Fortunately for you as a corporate leader, the collision of big data with new technology has created a perfect storm of possibility, making right now the most opportune time to perfect your sales incentives.

To a large extent, what's been achieved with compensation so far has been cultivated in the dark. Sure, you have theories about what drives the behavior of your employees, but you haven't found a way to truly quantify whether your tactics are working.

For years, companies have paid other companies for industry data or data from rival firms. But that information only gets you so far because it fails to measure the success of strategies at your own business.

Today, thanks to new technologies and the ubiquitous nature of the web, you're capable of using data to deliver this serious one-two punch to your overall strategy:

1. You'll understand the diverse composition of your sales force as it applies to motivation.

2. You'll fortify the incentive strategies with the historical and real-time data that reveals exactly what's needed to incent your team right.

Big data allows you to go well beyond simple compensation into areas of how pay in your organization impacts retention, engagement, quota attainment, and productivity. You can now ask deeper questions, get more detailed answers, and use what you've learned to build models that suit your unique needs.

For example, data can tell you that a top sales rep hasn't been quite up to par lately, and that his absenteeism rate has risen in the last quarter. You can dig deeply into your data to determine whether or not the behavior indicates sales rep turnover, and if so, what kind of incentives you could offer to reignite his motivation and thus retain him. Instead of just throwing more money at him, you can use data points like quota attainment and sales patterns to make more detailed decisions regarding the mix of compensation so that one of your best reps doesn't end up with the competition.

FIVE THINGS DATA TELLS YOU ABOUT YOUR SALES TEAM

Dig deep into your data to determine what employee behavior is telling you.

1. **What is the rate at which employees are progressing toward goals?** Look at how close employees are to meeting goals, as well as any related trends. For example do sales reps meet their quotas early in the cycle and then relax for the rest?

2. **Is employee engagement flagging?** If results aren't consistent, it might be time to spice up your incentive compensation plan.

3. **Is turnover imminent?** If your rock star rep is suddenly a middle performer, or if her absentee rate has climbed, she might be thinking about leaving the organization. Think about what you need to do to incent her to stay.

4. **Where could employee performance improve?** If reps are doing well with some objectives but not with others, it may be time to think about how well your compensation plan aligns with company goals.

5. **What are your best performers doing differently from the rest of your team?** Use the information to incent middle and low performers to kick it up a notch.

Although big data is out there, the typical organization lacks the resources to effectively run a simultaneous analysis on numerous large data streams. Cloud-based applications—resources available to businesses on demand via the Internet—provide the capabilities that leaders need to collect, analyze, and visualize complex data, and those same applications deliver effective solutions to the challenges of the three Vs that Doug Laney identified (you'll recall I mentioned them earlier in "Big Data Goes Mainstream"):

- **Velocity.** When data is created at high speeds, it's difficult to keep up with. To make the best decisions for your organization, you need access to up-to-the-minute data. Cloud-based solutions make sure that your data stream is in real time so you can build incentive compensation plans that work in the moment.

- **Variety.** Most organizations have many silos of data, each of which holds value when it comes to making the best strategic decisions. If the data is in different formats, however, finding accurate, usable information can feel like trying to find a particular grain of sand on an endless beach. Cloud-based apps put all your data in the same format, making management easier.

- **Volume.** Data grows at a rapid rate, and without the right tools it can quickly become disorganized. An in-house solution may not be capable of managing and holding all of your data in one area. Think of the place where your in-house data is stored as a closet. Once that closet is full, you need to find another storage place—or places. That means you'll need to remember what things you store in each nook and cranny, and who bothers with such inventorying! Otherwise, it's difficult to find the exact information you need. Cloud-based apps have unlimited storage and can expand as your data grows.

Between September and November 2012, the Aberdeen Group surveyed 312 end-user companies about their sales effectiveness, practices, and accomplishments. Aberdeen's research showed that top-performing companies are 32% more likely to integrate automated real-time compensation and quota data into their systems.[14]

Sales managers certainly have their work cut out for them in this data-driven, multigenerational society. But while big data may seem like a problem at first, look a little closer and you'll see it holds the solutions to positioning your diverse company to win. Are you convinced now that data is a friend, not a foe? In the next chapter, I'll show you exactly how to use data to improve engagement, productivity, and profits.

Visit www.GameThePlan.com to watch videos that share how to apply this chapter's principles in your own company.

CHAPTER 3

USE YOUR DATA KEY: UNLOCK THE DOOR TO EMPLOYEE ENGAGEMENT, PRODUCTIVITY, AND PROFITS

Famous nineteenth-century industrialist Andrew Carnegie once said, "Take away my factories, my plants; take away my railroads, my ships, my transportation, take away my money; strip me of all of these, but leave me my men, and in two or three years, I will have them all again."

Most business leaders would agree with Mr. Carnegie—employees hold the key to an organization's success. The impact of attracting, engaging, and retaining good employees is understood, but studies show we still have a lot of work to do in these areas.

A Gallup Employee Engagement Index shows that only 33% of workers are actively engaged, feeling connected to their company, and passionate about their work; 49% are non-engaged, punching

the clock without passion; and 18% are actively disengaged, dissatisfied enough to sabotage or undermine the efforts of coworkers and colleagues.[1]

According to a 2012 study conducted by Mercer, a global consulting leader in talent, engaging and retaining exceptional employees is at the top of the list of concerns for most organizations. What's more, twice as many companies are reporting reduced levels of employee engagement compared to just a couple of years ago.[2]

ENGAGED VS. HAPPY—WHAT'S THE DIFFERENCE?

Many organizations fail to understand the distinction between "happy" employees and "engaged" employees. Remember in chapter one I shared some examples of organizations that go above and beyond the norm to increase employee satisfaction— feeding staff grass-fed beef for lunch, offering on-site massages, giving extended sabbaticals? These fringe benefits are terrific, to be sure, and they probably *do* increase employee happiness. But how do they impact *engagement*?

In his book *Employee Engagement 2.0: How to Motivate Your Team for High Performance*, author Kevin E. Kruse explains the difference between engaged employees and happy employees. A company that prioritizes employee happiness may be disappointed when it doesn't result in engaged employees, he says. But organizations that focus on engagement first can expect happy employees.

He defines engagement as "the emotional commitment an employee has to the organization and its goals, resulting in the use of discretionary effort." Tactics like setting clear goals, communicating about how those goals will be met, and providing the help to see to it that objectives are met all increase employee engagement. Kruse says that an employee's discretionary effort results in what he calls the Engagement-Profit chain. Employees care more, so they are more productive, provide better service, and remain in their jobs longer. This type of behavior from employees leads to more sales and higher profits.[3] Ultimately, when employees feel positive emotions at work, Kruse says, those positive emotions spill into other areas of life.

BAD BOSS WORDS OF WISDOM

Sending employees mixed messages is a fast way to derail their engagement, and eventually their level of happiness. Your team looks to you as their boss to set an example, to be a good role model. That means your walk must match your talk. If you hear yourself saying any of the following lines, consider whether you are taking your own advice.

- **"I'm not a teacher, and you're not a student."** It's great to communicate to your staff that you consider yourself their equal. But when you follow this message with long-winded lectures or condescending corrections, your original sentiment means nothing.

- **"This isn't a hand slap."** When accompanied with a verbal dressing down, this statement means the opposite of what it intends. If you discipline a rep because he neglected to follow up with a crucial client, go ahead and call it a hand slap.

- **"You're the captain of your own ship."** A boss who purports not to be a micromanager shouldn't balk when team members take the initiative to make decisions. Letting your sales reps drive their own ships means loosening your grip on their projects.

- **"I'm too busy to read all my email."** Bosses who claim to be too busy to respond to communications come across as pompous. Usually managers offer this excuse in an attempt to weasel out of responsibility for dropping the ball. On the other hand, if you truly don't have time to read your messages, you need an administrative assistant.

- **"Own your slice of the pie."** This is a favorite of managers attempting to bully their subordinates into taking responsibility for mistakes. If you insist on your staff members owning up to their goof-ups, you must first show them that you will do the same. Bosses who don't practice what they preach alienate their staff.

- **"Take more proactive initiative!"** If you want your employees to progress beyond simply taking orders, don't treat them that way in the first place. Assistants fetch lunch and sort the bills; account executives and sales reps, on the other hand, already have their work cut out for them. Don't demean them by saddling them with menial chores. Instead, encourage initiative by providing autonomy, plenty of challenges, and room for growth.

Your words of wisdom only engage your staff if your behavior doesn't confuse them.

THE COST OF BOTH DISENGAGEMENT AND TURNOVER

Engagement and retention have been studied extensively—separately, as well as together as one concept. So there's no shortage of research when it comes to the impact of both on your organization, and how incentive plans factor into their attainment.

Consider these engagement and retention statistics, for example:

- The Towers Watson analysis of fifty global companies for its Global Workforce Study 2012 found that companies with low traditional engagement—engagement based on company goals and objectives, emotional connection, and willingness to go the extra mile—had an average operating margin of just under 10 percent. Those with high sustainable engagement—engagement based on being enabled to meet challenges and feeling energized—had operating margins at just over 27 percent—nearly three times higher. In a world where we are asking employees to do more with less, traditional engagement tactics no longer cut it. Today's employers must use modern resources and tools to enable workers while also figuring out what increases their physical, emotional, and social well-being. The study also revealed that 18 percent of highly engaged survey respondents said they were likely to leave their employer within the next two years, compared to 40 percent of disengaged employees.[4]

- The Gallup Employee Engagement Index I mentioned at the opening of this chapter revealed that actively disengaged employees—those who actually want to see their company fail—cost U.S. companies more than $300 billion per year in lost productivity.[5]

- The Center for American Progress looked at eleven research papers and found that replacing just one employee costs businesses, on average, about one-fifth of that employee's salary. The percentage increases with the person's salary and skill level; for instance, replacement costs at the senior level can be as high as 213 percent of that person's annual salary.[6]

THE LINK BETWEEN COMPENSATION AND ENGAGEMENT

Despite the dreary statistics about the high costs to a company when its employees are disengaged or choose to leave, the good news is that we *can* manage engagement and retention with the right approach. In a recent Engagement Index undertaken by Randstad, a global leader in HR services and staffing, compensation was one of the main drivers behind employee engagement: 36 percent of employees surveyed said bonuses and promotions were the most effective means of increasing their engagement.

According to the same report, however, *high* compensation does not necessarily equal *high* engagement. Instead, the research showed it was important to offer a variety of motivating tactics.[7] In this context, it's worth noting that highly compensated employees most likely did not arrive at their positions by slacking off. At one point during their careers, they were probably highly engaged. Lack of attention to incentives can result in a rep who is comfortable instead of one who is still hungry. A variety of well-mixed incentives will increase the appetite of the high-performing sales rep so the effects of complacency are no longer an issue.

According to a 2012 study of 312 companies conducted by Aberdeen, best-in-class companies said the top nonfinancial motivators were internal recognition for positive performance (57%), competition with other team members (35%), and learning and developing new skills (21%).[8]

Many organizations recognize the link between incentives and employee engagement and retention, spending more than a few hours attempting to develop incentive compensation programs that drive desired behaviors. But while their intentions are good, optimal employee engagement and retention still eludes many of these companies.

Why?

THE DIRTY DOZEN

Since Xactly was founded in 2005, I've worked with thousands of companies that were interested in improving their incentive compensation strategies. In helping them I've seen many mistakes, most made despite the companies' very good intentions. Here are the top twelve compensation plan mistakes I've identified over the years that turn those good intentions on their head—and thwart employee engagement and retention.

1. Weak Incentives

Weak plans, by which I mean those that provide small rewards as a portion of potential earnings and don't differentiate between low, medium, and high performers, have a larger impact on your best performers than you might believe. When incentives are weak—when the amount of effort or skill doesn't match the payout—your most talented sales reps can become discouraged and look for employment that offers stronger incentives.

Perhaps this is one of the reasons why poor performers are more satisfied than high performers are. When research and management consulting firm Leadership IQ studied three levels of performers at more than two hundred organizations, they found that in 42 percent of the companies, low performers were more engaged than were middle and high performers. If things like effort and talent are linked to outcome, it makes sense that this group would be more content. The payout, for this group, would feel more aligned to the outcome than it would for other groups.

Leadership IQ also found that low performers were more motivated to give 100 percent than high performers were, and more likely to recommend the company to potential employees than were high performers. They were more likely to feel like they were being held accountable for their performance than high performers were, and—here's the finding that should really give us pause—they were more likely to feel that all employees should live up to the same standards as high performers.[9]

This surprising study debunks the myth that the best performers are also the most engaged performers, and it should make you think twice about the way you're incenting your people. Most of us can stand to lose a few poor performers without negatively impacting our bottom line, but we simply cannot afford to lose our best workers. When incentives fail to differentiate between high and low performers, our best employees become unmotivated.

2. Unattainable Goals

Former GE CEO Jack Welch coined the term *stretch goals* to describe the process of asking employees to reach beyond what they think is possible to achieve extraordinary results. He put it this way: "By reaching for what appears to be the impossible, we often actually do the impossible. And even when we do not quite make it, we inevitably wind up doing much better than we would have done."[10]

Setting stretch goals is a great way to motivate employees to move outside their comfort zone, rise beyond mediocrity, and meet their full potential. According to information from Xactly's empirical database, a sales rep incentive attainment bell curve shows a spike at 100 percent of target incentives, with a drop-off as the percentage of quota attainment rises. Only about one-third of

Incentive Attainment vs. Quota Attainment

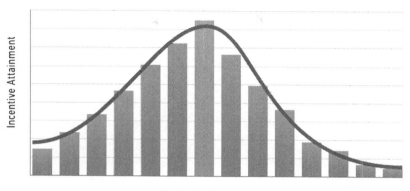

Quota Attainment

sales reps meet 120 percent or more of quota attainment. The data clearly shows that it's human nature to relax after goals are met, especially when the goals are very difficult to achieve. Runners who cross the finish line don't keep sprinting; they slow down because they know they've completed the race.

But when does an objective stop being a stretch goal and start being unattainable?

Managers who set stretch goals that they know are unattainable might not be concerned, ultimately, with their reps' ability to meet them. Even if reps fall short of meeting these unattainable goals, managers just might assume that they've reached their potential. In other words, managers who ask employees to jump twenty feet higher than needed are often happy when those employees jump only fifteen feet higher.

This approach fails to take into account that people want to succeed. No one wants to fail. When the bar is set so high that employees can't come close to it, they become discouraged and give up.

3. Easy Targets

Goals that are too easy to meet are equally problematic.

As I mentioned earlier, it's human nature to relax when goals are met. If a bar is set too low, not only will you never know what your sales team is truly capable of, but you'll also fail to optimize productivity and profits.

Easy targets create a sense of entitlement among workers that can be difficult to shake. In this case, when you do increase goals—whether it's to stay in business or because you realize the current target structure is breeding mediocrity—you'll likely be met with resistance. Easy targets train employees to believe they are owed something just for showing up.

Simple targets may also incent employees to put their own needs before the needs of the company or their customers. I've heard from companies that have provided short-term incentives to sales reps only to find that those reps then influence the timing of sales to gain the greatest personal benefit. And such reps may achieve quota well before the incentive period ends and then check out. If reps don't need the whole incentive period to meet quota, they have time on their hands to game the system. One surefire way to fix this problem is to make targets more challenging.

4. One-Size-Fits-All Incentives

There is no one-size-fits-all incentive plan good enough to drive the desired behaviors of all individuals or groups within an organization. To think so is to misunderstand the complexities behind how individuals and groups operate.

Stanford University recently did a study on how to motivate two different cultural groups to act interdependently. They found that in order to motivate those in the first group to act for the greater good, it was necessary to emphasize and appeal to their *independence*. Those in the second cultural group, on the other hand, found appeals to act interdependently or independently equally motivating. Ultimately, the experiment showed that the motivation to act is deeply tied to cultural context.[11]

As I discussed in chapter two, if you're incenting your Gen Y workers the same way you're incenting your Baby Boomer employees, you're not getting the best results from either. Each generational group has unique needs and desires. Until you take the time to tap into these differences and gain insight on the exact drivers of desired results, you're motivating in the dark.

SURVEY SAYS: A 10% RAISE AND A $1,000 BONUS MIGHT BE A GREAT IDEA. OR A NOT SO GREAT IDEA

In 2010, Google made headlines when someone leaked to the media that every Google employee had received a $1,000 holiday bonus and would get a 10% raise effective the first of the new year.[12]

When you consider that Google had just about 20,000 employees at the time, many earning high salaries, quick math tells you that this plan wasn't cheap. In fact, it was very generous. No doubt, Google dug deep into its pockets to make employees happy.

What happened next wasn't so surprising. As media outlet after media outlet picked up the story, online readers chimed in with their opinions. The overwhelming consensus was that Google was giving us a breath of fresh air among the smog of belt-tightening and layoffs. Comments like, "I wish I worked for Google!" were common.

But then something odd happened. Internet critics started pointing out why this incredibly sweet deal might not be so sweet after all. These critics pointed out that high performers hitting it out of the park should find the plan unfair, because they were getting the same as low performers who hadn't contributed nearly enough to the organization.

I don't tell this story to give my opinion on the Google plan, which I don't know the details of. I tell it to illustrate that what's inspiring to one might not be inspiring to all. Reader comments make one realize that compensation and benefits policies must be designed thoughtfully, that is, taking into consideration the message they give to *all* employees.

Incentives are the primary motivators of employee behaviors. Failure to consider the different needs of individual members and groups when designing incentive plans significantly reduces the power of motivation, frequently drives the wrong behavior, and can mean the difference between successfully lifting off the ground or crashing on the runway.

5. Lack of Recognition

While financial incentives may attract top talent to your organization, recognition and rewards keep them there. According to a *McKinsey Quarterly* survey of 1,047 executives, managers, and employees from around the world, respondents rated the non-cash incentive of recognition higher than cash bonuses, increased base pay, and stock or stock options.[13]

Yet many incentive plans ignore this key element, or they reward a couple of their top sales performers once a quarter and then call it a day.

The key to tapping into the "recognition culture" lies in finding ways to sincerely recognize and reward *all* employees. That means not only recognizing their unique talents and contributions but also recognizing them in ways that are meaningful *to them*. (Revisit chapter two for more about tactical ways you can do this.) Lack of recognition often translates to lack of appreciation, and no one likes to be either underappreciated or totally unappreciated. If you have a high turnover rate, or if employees gripe and produce results that indicate their lack of engagement, your lack of targeted recognition may be to blame.

SOMETIMES, MOTIVATION REQUIRES REDEFINITION

At Xactly, our reps are constantly teaching us how to better motivate them. One of the hallmarks of our compensation strategy is that we are willing to be flexible and learn as we go along, adapting our plans to the reps they're designed for.

Case in point: When one of our Gen Y account executives from our Small Business team boldly asked for a promotion after hitting quota for two straight quarters, we were at first shocked. But we listened. This AE truly believed that he had demonstrated sufficient positive performance to merit a pretty significant reward.

We knew the rep wasn't ready to be promoted beyond his AE role after only six months, but we heard what he was really asking: to be recognized and rewarded for his efforts quickly. So we came up with a progressive solution that divided the AE role into two Small Business team subroles:

SMB1 and SMB2

We then created multiple growth stages for each subrole:

Junior < Senior < Team Lead < Mentor

All eight subroles now have clear responsibilities, expectations, and benchmarks that must be reached in order for a rep to progress to the next growth stage. Small Business team AEs have seven possible "promotions" ahead of them before they are eventually promoted beyond their AE role, and we've even created a training program to lead our reps through the growth stages of SMB1 and SMB2.

By giving our AEs clearly defined benchmarks and then rewarding them promptly with a move up the stage ladder, we motivate our linear-minded Gen Y reps better. The Gen Yer whose request instigated this new system was thrilled about the prospect of so much growth potential, and he has gone on to become one of our company's top-performing sales reps.

6. Capping Commissions

Employees who are paid a commission should feel like *they* are in a win-win situation. The more money they make for your organization, the more money they should be paid. It's as simple as that.

INCENTING WITH GOOD INTENTION

"I have never felt so appreciated at any other company."
—Cassie Desmarais

Cassie Desmarais is an executive assistant at The Lakeside Group, a Cleveland-based executive search firm. A shining example of an employee who loves her job, Cassie is particularly delighted with her employer's incentive plan, which goes way beyond monetary bonuses. You might be surprised why.

When she was hired, Cassie received a thank-you card and a box of chocolate-covered strawberries. "It was a great feeling. They went out of their way to show their appreciation," says Cassie. "I should have been the one thanking *them* for giving me such a great opportunity!" Her employers continued to show their appreciation with more gourmet treats and even an all-expenses-paid, four-day trip to Las Vegas. These thoughtful, personal gestures help cement Cassie's ongoing loyalty.

Because Cassie guides the interview process and helps to find the best candidates, she gets a bonus each time a candidate is hired. She also receives quarterly and annual incentives. When you consider her enthusiasm and commitment to her job, you can imagine that she helps secure higher numbers of quality candidates than a lackluster peer might, and that ultimately drives up company revenue.

But many organizations cap commission plans after a certain point. For example, they reduce incentives after employees meet 120 percent of their goals. Some of these companies want employees to knock it out of the park, but at the same time they're uncomfortable with the thought of those employees making more than their managers do. Others want to hedge their bets in case the compensation plan turns out to be poorly designed and they end up paying too much for too little work.

Remember, your compensation plan drives the behavior you seek. Capped commission plans sabotage your efforts to motivate your sales force, sending employees a message to stop trying once they've reached a certain level. Plans that are capped too soon also tell employees that you're not looking out for their best interest, which can result in feelings of mistrust. They might think, *Sure, you'll reward me for hard work, but only up to a certain point.* In a sense, you're telling them that *you* ultimately control their success.

Here's the deal: If you've designed a broken compensation plan or if you're unsure about how paying employees the maximum amount will affect your bottom line, focus on a remedy and study your numbers. (See the section titled "Clean Up Your Act with Data: The 7-Step Plan to Scrubbing Your Incentives, Kicking Up Engagement, and Keeping Great Employees" that follows this list of the Dirty Dozen for how to find a remedy.) Remember: Your employees shouldn't have to pay the price. If your plan is well designed, focus on helping your star employees continue to shine. Don't be concerned about paying them what they've earned—even when they've earned more than their managers did.

7. Failure to Understand Sales Deal Spending

According to the *Harvard Business Review*, U.S. organizations spend more than $800 billion on sales force compensation every year—more than *three times* the amount spent on advertising. This, the single largest investment for most B2B companies, is three times more than what companies spend on advertising.[14]

Yet, most of us seem to spend more time thinking about advertising than about sales force compensation. Let me help you put that in perspective. Imagine you are playing a game in which you are being timed to find two figures:

1. The cost of Chrysler's 2011 Super Bowl advertisement featuring Eminem; and

2. The amount your organization spent on compensation in the same year.

Which figure is more easily found? If the cost of the most expensive Super Bowl ad in history isn't already burned into your brain, a thirty-second search on the Internet will tell you it cost about $12 million. I would be willing to bet that determining the cost of your compensation plan will take you considerably longer. Why? Because, when pressed, many leaders are in the dark regarding incentive compensation plan spending. You might be surprised, but some CEOs have no idea how many checks are cut for a single sales deal, how payment is determined, and whether commissions complement the levels of contribution.

You might likewise be surprised to find that, on average (and according to Xactly's empirical data), about fourteen different checks are written for every sales deal. Many organizations split incentives without taking level of contribution into consideration, sometimes paying people no longer involved in the deal, which creates flimsy ties between the incentive and the action.

Ultimately, an organization that doesn't understand how money is expended on sales deals can't drive specific actions, and it fails to engage and motivate employees.

8. Inaccurate, Outdated Measurements

You've gathered an impressive team of employees and developed an incentive plan designed to push productivity into high gear. The next step is to track and analyze certain plan measurements to determine how you can make your plan even better.

This sounds like a fairly easy, straightforward process until you consider that the metrics associated with market share—employee revenue, cost of a sale, close rates, and customer profitability—are often inaccurate or outdated. Sometimes the information is gathered from several different sources of truth, while other times it's simply erroneous—the result of spreadsheet errors or a manual process gone awry.

According to a 2012 Aberdeen Group study of 312 organizations that measured sales effectiveness, practices, and accomplishments, organizations that use automatic incentive compensation tools reported that 54% of first-year reps met quota, compared to 43% of first-year reps from companies not using the software.[17]

Inaccurate and outdated measurements won't motivate success or deliver the results you want. Simply put, if you're using the wrong metrics to drive behavior, you'll get results based on those metrics. In other words, you'll end up driving the wrong behavior.

9. Using Too Many Metrics

When it comes to measuring employee performance, less means more. If you're using more than three metrics to measure performance, your organization may be suffering from *incentive plan obesity*. The term, coined by IBM executives in the mid-1990s, was used to describe an incentive plan that had sales reps juggling twenty different performance measures.[18]

Too many metrics results in a lack of prioritization and a lack of direction, and employees are left wondering what's *really* required to receive rewards and accurate payouts. Metrics overkill sends this message: "We don't really know what we want to reward! So just

SPREADSHEET ERRORS HEARD ROUND THE WORLD

In 2013, the U.S. Department of Labor issued a somber announcement along with its first-quarter employment cost index: A technical mistake made during the data collection phase resulted in an error that caused the previous three quarters of employment compensation data to be wrong.[15]

Oops.

This announcement was made just weeks after what many journalists dubbed "the spreadsheet error heard round the world," when a grad student discovered a simple spreadsheet error that substantiated the conclusions in a paper by Harvard economists Carmen Reinhart and Kenneth Rogoff. The formula error skewed debt to growth stats, possibly resulting in decisions to slash government spending despite high unemployment. As a result, columnist Paul Krugman asked, "So, did an Excel coding error destroy the economies of the Western world?"[16]

What's the relationship between these spreadsheet failures and the failures of your incentive compensation plan? Formula errors in your spreadsheets can result in incorrect information. If you use spreadsheet-based information to make decisions, your incentive plan may not work as desired.

Today there are new, technologically advanced methods of gathering compensation data, but some leaders still prefer to put on their old, comfortable shoes and walk down the familiar path of gathering data from spreadsheets and manual systems.

Sure, your spreadsheet use probably won't cause the international havoc mentioned above, but it won't provide you with the tools you need to motivate your employees either. Not only do compensation errors affect an organization's bottom line and de-motivate sales reps; outdated data based on faulty math or formulas makes it almost impossible to demystify the info you need to tap into human psychology and develop plans that drive desired behaviors.

go out there and do a lot of things well, and who knows, maybe it will work out for you!"

This lack of direction impacts employee control, and eventually it leads to frustration. Employees don't know where to focus their attention, don't trust the system, and aren't sure they are being rewarded fairly. Also, more metrics leaves more opportunities to game the plan. Employees in this situation will put up with the confusion only for so long before they beat a path to the door.

YOU CAN'T MOTIVATE AN INDIVIDUALIST WITH GROUP BONUSES

In the airline industry, pilot unions have rules that prohibit pilots from being paid for individual performance. One major national airline tried to circumvent this rule by launching a bonus profit-sharing program to encourage pilots to use less fuel. For instance, a pilot taxiing on a runway can choose to shut off his engine. The airline got around the union restrictions by rewarding pilots as a group, not individually.

In theory, the plan made sense, but in practice, it failed. As any restaurant server would probably tell you, shared bonuses aren't always a great way to motivate individual behavior. As a whole, the pilots didn't respond well to the group incentive. In fact, a pilot friend of mine told me that some of his colleagues thought the incentive so worthless they intentionally fired up their engines when they didn't have to as a form of protest. That's how firmly they believed that their tiny part in saving fuel would not make an impact on the overall bonus.

My friend believes that individual bonuses would help lower fuel usage, but despite sharing his belief with airline management, no change was made. I wonder what would happen if the airline industry incorporated more effective compensation strategies.

10. Poor Territory Management

Ah, the tedious task of territory management. Leaders of sales teams spend tons of administrative time defining and assigning territories, yet still struggle with visibility, accuracy, and timeliness.

If sales resources across well-defined territories aren't aligned and managed in real time, daily business challenges won't be met. You might not have the right coverage as territory needs change, employees might not be assigned to the most appropriate territories, and workloads might be unbalanced because of that.

According to the Aberdeen study mentioned previously, top-performing companies are 23% more likely to use management technologies to develop quotas and territories for their reps, resulting in a sizable book of business for all reps.[19]

In addition, lack of teamwork among the sales, finance, and operations departments causes late and inaccurate payments. The result? You lose opportunity *and* your best employees.

11. Delayed Gratification

Too much time between effort and payment leads to poor focus, lack of engagement, and dissatisfaction.

In the 1960s, Stanford University released a study on self-control known today as "the marshmallow test." The test asked a simple question: Will a preschooler eat one marshmallow now, or hold out and be rewarded with two later?[20]

Some children were able to delay gratification by using amusing distraction tactics, such as sitting on the marshmallow, thus keeping it out of sight and out of mind. Others were too tempted by the sugary goodness and gobbled theirs up right away. But regardless of individual reactions, all these kids had one thing in common—they wanted the marshmallow *right then and there.*

Your sales reps aren't preschoolers, but they don't appreciate large lag times between earning their rewards and receiving them. You can force them to "sit on the marshmallow" if you like, but when employees put their rewards out of sight and out of mind, those rewards are no longer being used to drive behavior. Sure, you'll always have some employees who are willing to delay gratification. But if one of your competitors offers to let them eat the marshmallow as soon as they've earned it, you can bet your employee will take them up on the offer.

12. Failure to Change with the Times

When the *Harvard Business Review* published an article exploring why people resist change, the two reasons that topped the list were uncertainty and the inability to let go of comfortable routines.[21]

Face it—most people would rather stay in their current, familiar situation than walk off into the unknown. Even if it means they remain stuck in a less-than-ideal situation.

And, since people—who as a species tend to eschew change—are the ones running organizations, it comes as no surprise that change often comes too little, too late, especially in the area of incentive compensation. Leaders often stick with what's worked in the past, blaming poorly performing employees or forces outside management's control when current plans no longer motivate like they used to.

The fact is, of course, that the only constant in business is change. Internal changes, such as the introduction of a new product or changing customer needs, and external forces, such as new competition, changing technology, or a shifting economy, both call for a change in company strategy.

Keep it simple: When company strategy changes, so should your incentive compensation plan. If you're doing the same thing over and over again and it's not working, don't expect different results. If you don't respond to changing internal and external conditions, motivation and retention will decrease, and you'll pay the price in hard numbers.

CLEAN UP YOUR ACT WITH DATA: THE 7-STEP PLAN TO SCRUBBING YOUR INCENTIVES, KICKING UP ENGAGEMENT, AND KEEPING GREAT EMPLOYEES

Your past and present data gives you ample information about how you can fix the twelve problem areas I just discussed. All you need is access to an accurate, single source of real-time information to deliver an incentive compensation plan that motivates sales employees to do their best work *and* to stick around.

No, I'm not talking about digging through spreadsheets or other manual systems. Advances in technology and the introduction of automated sales performance management software make it easier than ever to find the information you're looking for.

To improve your organization's engagement and retention, I advocate using your data in seven key steps.

Step #1: Think short term. Begin by looking at the impact of your incentive plan this year, and then take another look by quarter. If you're meeting company goals, you're incenting the right employee behaviors. If you're falling short of your goals, analyze your data to identify problem areas.

THE COLOR CONUNDRUM

Consumers' mouths water when an electronic product comes in a range of bright color choices. But for retailers, stocking one product in multiple hues can cause inventory overload.

One electronics retailer, MicroWarehouse, carried a popular electronic device that came in a small variety of candy colors: red, orange, or blue. The manufacturer insisted on shipping the product in equal amounts of each color, so every time MicroWarehouse ordered more red and blue devices, they received more orange ones too. The problem? The orange product wasn't moving. Shoppers simply preferred red and blue, leaving the orange ones on the shelves.

Inventory that doesn't move is death for retailers, so MicroWarehouse came up with a sales incentive: Every time a rep sold an orange device, he received a SPIF bonus of $100. The incentive motivated the sales team, and quickly the orange products started to move! This was great for MicroWarehouse too. While the candy-colored devices certainly looked delicious, MicroWarehouse did not want to have to eat their inventory.

Step #2: Look ahead. Use historical data to look at trends over multiple years. A historical review will show you when a formerly tried-and-true plan stopped driving the desired behaviors and results, and you can use that information to make plan changes. If the data shows that your former high-flyers are slacking, or if you're experiencing higher-than-normal turnover, you know that your incentive compensation plan has gone stale. A long-term review of your data may also indicate when specific internal or external factors caused a need for a plan strategy change, so you can figure out ahead of time how to react to these factors and avoid problems.

SPIF OR SPIFF. WHAT'S THE DIF (DIFF)?

A Special Performance Incentive Fund, more commonly known by the acronym SPIF, is a short-term sales incentive typically used to drive sales results that are needed right now. It's probably no coincidence that the verb to *spiff* means to dress or spruce up something and give it a little extra pizzazz. In the same way that you can spiff up your appearance, you can spiff up your incentive plan.

I have no idea if the first person who coined the term SPIF came up with the phrase first and the acronym followed, or chose the acronym based on the verb and went from there. But one thing I do know is that a well-thought-out SPIF can make any incentive plan feel, well, a little *spiffier*.

Since all companies have short-term goals, SPIFs should be a regular part of your incentive compensation strategy. As a matter of fact, recent research from the Aberdeen Group showed that more than 50% of best-in-class companies drove their increased profits through SPIFs.[22]

When spiffing up your incentive plan with SPIFs, keep these six things in mind:

1. Know your goal. Is your short-term goal to boost revenue, units sold, sales leads, or order size? Having a solid handle on your goal will help you develop SPIFs that drive the behaviors necessary to meet goals.

2. Be unpredictable. SPIFs that come at the same time every month or year can be taken advantage of by sales reps. Keep your plan "gameable" by introducing SPIFs at unforeseeable times, and be sure you don't have so many SPIFs throughout the year that gaming them becomes the main focus. As a good rule of thumb, you should have no more than six to eight SPIFs in one year.

3. Figure out your time frame. Determine whether your short-term needs are a week, a month, a quarter, or a year.

4. Keep it simple. SPIFs should provide guaranteed results for specific actions, and both results and actions should be crystal clear. Sales reps should understand that if they sell X they will be rewarded with $Y.

5. Target your audience. One of the greatest benefits of short-term incentives that are quickly deployed is that they can be easily tailored to individuals and groups. Use your data to determine what kind of SPIFs have worked in the past and which are likely to work in the future, then use predictive modeling to determine potential outcomes.

6. Analyze the outcome. Compare results to your predicted outcome and decide if you like what you see. If your SPIF didn't drive the desired behavior, use your data to figure out why. Then tweak your plan.

Step #3: Differentiate. There's no need for ineffective, one-size-fits-all plans. With single-source, up-to-the-minute data, you know which incentives work for one group, and which don't. You can even determine whether group or individual incentives make the most sense. If there is a balance of individual work and teamwork, the data helps you determine how incentives should be weighed in different combinations, depending upon the situation.

Step #4: Balance. Data shows you when incentives are too strong or too weak, so you can balance them. If top performers aren't performing as well as usual, or if employees are going to competitors, check your data to see if you're providing small rewards as a portion of potential earnings, and then fix the problem by providing stronger incentives. On the other hand, if data indicates that strong incentives aren't working as well as you think they should, take a look at your metrics. Make sure you're providing simple, well-defined desired outcomes closely tied to measurable performance employees can control.

Step #5: Align and appreciate. How rewards are structured and communicated have an impact on engagement. Identify performance and competency expectations, communicate expectations to employees, and use hard data to determine how well expectations are being met. Clarify desired skills and behaviors by rewarding the right actions as soon as possible so gratification isn't delayed and there's a direct tie between performance and pay.

Step #6: Provide visibility. Improve teamwork, build trust, and kick employees into high competitive gear by giving them access to their own data. Visibility not only enables employees to see how close they are to meeting their goals, it also gives them the peace of mind of knowing that their paychecks, commissions, and bonuses are correct.

Step #7: Review. Review your data on a regular basis to determine the efficacy of your incentive compensation plan. What works now may not work later. What works for one employee may not work for others. If engagement and retention aren't as good as they should be, use data to identify problems, learn from your mistakes, and adjust your plan.

———

Data is the key that unlocks the mix of incentives that increases engagement, makes certain your best employees stay put, and boosts productivity and profits. But there are several different types of data. In the next chapter we'll discuss three types of data and tell you which kind you'll need to access to *really* make a difference.

Visit www.GameThePlan.com to watch videos that share how
to apply this chapter's principles in your own company.

CHAPTER 4

THE THREE-LEGGED STOOL: ADD A POWER PUNCH TO ACADEMIC AND ANECDOTAL INFORMATION WITH EMPIRICAL DATA

In June 2013, Nik Wallenda—seventh-generation aerialist of the Flying Wallendas—walked across a chasm just east of the Grand Canyon on a two-inch steel cable. The cable stretched the length of four football fields from one side to the other, at a height equal to that of the Empire State Building. There was no net below him, no safety harness to prevent him from plummeting to the earth if he lost his balance.

As if this daredevil stunt weren't nerve-wracking enough, historical information shared by Discovery Channel hosts increased the anxiety of the thirteen million people who tuned in to watch: Nik's great-grandfather, Karl Wallenda, had fallen to his death attempting a similar stunt in 1978.

But as Nik Wallenda stepped onto the wire, I had confidence in him. He had spent his entire life preparing for moments like this, and I knew he wasn't relying solely on one type of data to prepare for the stunt. Instead, he was using three types of data to build a strong, stable three-legged stool. He used academic data to determine how the wire should be set up and weighted; he used anecdotal data—details he had gathered from observing his own performances throughout the years—to reduce risks; and he had lots of empirical evidence—data collected through the study and analysis of how he, his family, and other aerialists had performed in similar situations—to support his effort.

To prepare himself for any situation, Nik trained in his Sarasota, Florida, hometown during Tropical Storm Andrea, which produced wind gusts of fifty-two miles per hour and torrential downpours. When Mother Nature didn't provide difficult circumstances in which to train, he broke out a wind machine and cranked it up to ninety-one miles per hour. He also learned to manage the subtleties of the wire itself, getting a feel for tensions and rhythms and understanding when he should slow down, speed up, or adjust the size of his steps.[1] He had closely examined the data in just about any potential situation and knew what to expect and how to react to stay safe.

I'm about to make the parallel here to the world of compensation. Until now, business executives have relied on academic data and anecdotal data to develop incentive strategies and plans. Consequently, they've had varied results because developing compensation plans without empirical data is like walking on a tightrope totally unaware of the dangers you may encounter and thus having no plan for dealing with them. That's reckless! Some organizations have gotten lucky; their compensation plans have gotten them to the other side. Far more organizations, however, have lost their balance and stumbled.

Designing your company's incentive compensation plan shouldn't feel like a daredevil stunt. Like Nik Wallenda, you should have the evidence behind you to feel confident about staying on your feet. In this chapter, I'll show you how to add empirical data to the academic and anecdotal data you've already gathered to do just that.

ACADEMIC, ANECDOTAL, EMPIRICAL. WHAT'S THE DIFFERENCE?

Organizations use three types of data to develop and improve incentive compensation.

1. **Academic data,** which is found in studies and surveys. Many universities, as well as industry organizations, have done comprehensive research on what does and doesn't motivate sales staff.

2. **Anecdotal data,** which is gathered through your own experience. For example, a manager who has been leading sales teams knows, to some degree, what has worked in the past Similarly, a sales compensation consultant knows from experience what incentives perform best for companies in certain industries.

3. **Empirical data,** in which results of specific situations are gathered through systematic collection techniques, then studied and analyzed. f you want to know how a sales staff typically behaves in a specific situation, well-organized empirical data can tell you. Empirical data can be difficult to gather and arrange, but when used correctly it is some of the most valuable data available.

THE GOOD, THE BAD, AND THE UGLY: THE PROS AND CONS OF ACADEMIC AND ANECDOTAL INFORMATION

CFOs, sales leaders, human resources professionals, and others who develop incentive compensation plans must clear three hurdles:

1. Identify organizational goals;

2. Identify the behavior that will help the company reach those goals; and

3. Identify the mix of compensation that will reinforce behaviors needed to meet corporate goals.

Data is both the muscle and the speed that will help compensation planners clear these hurdles. Data provides the historical context of what motivated sales teams in the past, the current context of what motivates teams in the present, and the basis for projecting what might motivate sales teams in the future.

Universities, independent researchers, compensation consulting firms, human resources organizations, and even individual companies in many different industries have done lots of good research in an effort to build incentive compensation plans that help organizations attract and retain top-notch employees, meet goals, and stay competitive.

The types of surveys that yield such scholastic data are thoughtfully designed, and the selection of jobs to be surveyed and the identification of target participants are very carefully considered. To get the data they are looking for, survey designers think about the specific employee groups covered, the breadth and depth of functional areas to be represented, and the hierarchical levels that will be included.[2]

Academic data, when it comes from a well-designed survey, is quite valuable. It can get to the heart of "best practices" and can tell you how other companies of your size and in your industry or geographic location are paying their sales reps, so you can compete.

Although academic data serves as a necessary jumping-off point, it's also limited. It may tell you what incentives have worked in similar companies, but it doesn't tell you how incentives have worked in *your* company. It's simply impossible to find a survey sample that's representative of your exact goals and your exact workforce.

Most organizations use anecdotal data gathered from their own experiences to support academic data. For example, if you've been a sales leader for two decades, and thus have a good "feel" for what motivates sales teams, you know what's worked in the past for specific people in specific situations. But while your experience is valuable, relying on it to design your incentive compensation plans is risky at best. There's no way to guarantee that what has worked in the past will work in the present. Plus, what has worked for one group may not work for another. For example, what incents your top-notch sales reps may not work for the rest of the reps. Goals, culture, and demographics may have shifted or may be in the process of shifting. The gamification plan you introduced that encouraged your Millennial sales team to crush it at your last organization, for instance, may not work at your present company, which is more heavily populated with Gen Xers.

Are academic and anecdotal data worth considering? Yes. I think both serve a purpose and are necessary ingredients in the design of any incentive compensation plan. But if you want to build a solid compensation plan that won't tip over, you need to add a third leg—empirical data—to your stool.

THE (POSSIBLE) MIRACLE OF EMPIRICAL DATA

Show me a company's comp plan, and I'll show you how the employees behave.
—Jack Welch

The idea of using empirical data to improve incentive compensation plans has been around for some time. In 1996, Canice John Prendergast, of the University of Chicago Booth School of Business, wrote a paper for the National Bureau of Economic Research titled "What Happens within Firms? A Survey of Empirical Evidence on Compensation Policies." In this paper, Prendergast argues that lack of empirical information hampers our understanding of incentive compensation. He questions the effectiveness of how different compensation plans were studied at the time, particularly whether comparing the productivity of different plans reflected the omitted variables more than the effects of the plans themselves.

Aggregate data collected on employees at many different organizations is certainly helpful, he said, but this data answers only a limited set of questions. In order to answer a more comprehensive set of questions, Prendergast argued, you would need to collect data on the *specific plans*. Only when this type of empirical data is collected can you directly relate productivity to specific types of incentive plans. And that's where empirical data makes its entrance.[3]

Empirical data enables comp plan developers to accurately understand and measure employee behavior and then use this understanding to develop custom-tailored incentive compensation plans that align with company goals, increase employee motivation, and, ultimately, improve business results.

Getting to the Bottom of Behavior

Many organizations simplify motivation, believing that if employees are hungry they'll do anything to reach for the big carrot dangling in front of them. But the truth is much more complicated.

In November 2005, the Federal Reserve Bank of Boston sponsored a study conducted by MIT, the University of Chicago, and Carnegie Mellon. The results were published in a paper titled "Large Stakes and Big Mistakes."

The study asked a group of students to perform a variety of tasks, from throwing a ball to solving equations and word puzzles. Researchers offered three levels of monetary rewards related to low performance, mid-level performance, and high performance.

When subjects were asked to complete purely mechanical tasks, higher pay resulted in higher performance. These results were hardly surprising. But when cognitive skill was needed to complete a task, a larger reward led to *worse* performance. These results were surprising, leading researchers of this study and of others to think about how intrinsic motivation—that based on taking pleasure in the activity or being recognized for the activity, rather than that based on tangible rewards like money—contributes to productivity.[4] And there we arrive at the crux of *why* understanding employee behavior is so important. If former topnotch reps are barely making quota or leaving for your competitors, their behavior indicates that something is currently amiss in the land of incentives.

The right data can tell you (1) which employees might benefit from coaching and training, (2) which might need an injection of gamification in their incentive package to ramp up competition, (3) which might require more recognition, and (4) which might require a different mix of incentives to engage in the behavior you need to meet corporate goals. It can tell you whether you're falling short in areas of quota, margin, or territory optimization so that you can focus your incentives there.

Understanding how employees behave in certain situations, and what motivates them, allows you to adjust your incentive compensation plan so that *their* behavior helps you reach *your* goals. Similar to the GPS in an automobile, empirical data tells you where you've been, the route you've taken to get there, and the roads you must drive in order to reach your destination. If you take a wrong turn, no worries; your data, just like that GPS system, can quickly and accurately measure current employee behavior in order for you to "recalculate" your route and get back on the right track.

Until just recently, it was difficult to collect the kind of data needed to really get a bead on employee behavior. The types of tools Prendergast and other scholarly researchers had at their disposal to collect data on both performance measures and incentive plans offered to employees were limited and subjective. Today, technological advances have made it possible to collect the empirical data we need to strengthen our three-legged stool.

TECH BACK THE NIGHT: GETTING REAL RESULTS IN REAL TIME

You have the ability to build—and tap into—your own empirical database. Any historical or current data you have—whether it pertains to quotas or territories, performance or pay—can be carefully analyzed and studied so you can make decisions that help your organization meet its objectives.

Before you break out your incentive compensation software and dig into your data, you need to know exactly what you're trying to achieve. Are you trying to improve revenue or profit? Do you want to gain a bigger piece of market share? Are you looking to improve customer service? Do you hope to bring in more or bigger accounts? Decide what matters to you. Measure what matters. Then, build or refine your incentive plan based on that data.

Here are eight things you can do with empirical data:

1. **Realign Your Sales Territories**

   Most sales managers would agree that sales territory misalignment probably contributes to the $500 billion that American organizations waste on sales productivity costs every year.[5] Aligning territories without data is like trying to piece together a giant jigsaw puzzle without having a picture to guide you. Just when you think you've figured out how to balance workloads among reps, how to increase motivation by providing the right incentives, or how to increase sales, something changes—your customers, your sales force, or your competition. Good data can help you predict these changes, and the study and analysis of similar situations in the past can help you come up with an effective response to them.

   In their paper titled "Sales Territory Alignment: An Overlooked Productivity Tool" for the Kellogg School of Business, Andris A. Zoltners and Sally E. Lorimer write that companies often fail to realign their territories because they feel they don't have the *right* data.[6] Today, that's no longer a valid excuse. The data from your incentive compensation software can help you assess the sales potential of territories and customers, balance territories to provide equal incentives to all sales reps, and design territories to save money and maximize coverage.

2. **Improve Quota Attainment**

   In his May 8, 2011, post in *The Sales & Marketing Effectiveness Blog*, Ryan Tognazzini talks about what he calls the "panic-euphoria continuum."[7] You know, that roller coaster that a sales rep rides as she asks herself, "Am I going to make my numbers?" The answer can change by the minute, the hour, the day, or the week.

Fortunately, the use of empirical data takes the emotions out of quota attainment by making the answer to the above questions more predictably, a yes. Empirical data from your incentive compensation software enables you to easily conduct a win/loss analysis, as well as determine whether adjustments are needed to smooth out the revenue stream, or shorten time periods to help reps hit or exceed their quotas.

3. Set Attainable Goals

When the bar is set too low, you miss out on revenue. When the bar is set too high, reps give up. The goal, then, is to set the bar high, but not so high that goals aren't attainable.

Data from your incentive compensation system can tell you when the quota is too high or too low, enabling you to change sales rep behavior by identifying and offering incentives for attainable stretch goals.

4. Reward the Right Contributors, the Right Way

Are you spending most of your time thinking about how to incent your Hunters—those who close the deal—while failing to think about how you're compensating the rest of the team? Big mistake. Your Hunters wouldn't be able to do their jobs without the sales support specialists who draw up proposals or present complicated demos, or the Prospectors who find good leads and fill the pipeline.

Information from Xactly's own empirical database shows that about fourteen checks are cut for every sales deal. An assessment of your data can tell you who is getting paid, how they contribute to the deal, and whether the ways they are getting paid incent the behavior you're looking for.

5. **Build Better Managers**

Would you rather have excellent salespeople and a mediocre sales manager, or an excellent sales manager in charge of average salespeople? It's a tough question, but the truth is, excellent sales managers are capable of getting the most out of average or below-average salespeople, while even the best sales teams can fail under a poor manager.

Your empirical data can help sales managers go from good to great by giving them access to reports, dashboards, and metrics in real time, so they can focus their efforts in the right places. Automated systems also take the struggle out of territory and goal setting by providing the highest level of visibility and management insight.

6. **Manage Top, Middle, and Low Performers**

Data from your incentive compensation software can measure individual performance, from the CEO all the way down to sales staff at the bottom of the hierarchy. You can dig deeply into your proprietary empirical data to answer questions such as, *How good is this individual?* and *How has this individual succeeded?* If the behavior of the individual or of a team of individuals is not driving the results you want, you know it's time to take another look at your incentive compensation plan.

Examining the data will tell you (1) where you need to focus your training, (2) when to expect turnover, (3) when it's time to introduce a SPIF or another type of bonus to create engagement, (4) how long it takes a newly hired rep to start producing, and (5) when it's time to let a rep go.

7. **Boost Productivity with Immediate Feedback**

Individual data that can be easily accessed via a dashboard in real time tells reps exactly how far away they are from attaining their individual quotas and how a particular deal will impact them financially. This type of immediate feedback taps into the human desire to be rewarded, and real-time visibility drives competitive behavior.

8. **Move Beyond Financial Incentives**

The paper Prendergast wrote in 1996 proved money ain't everything, and that holds true today. Empirical data in your incentive compensation system can tell you when financial incentives alone aren't working, and when and where you should add intrinsic motivators, such as recognition, autonomy, and gamification. Use your data to build a variety of incentives, and then reward individuals and teams the moment they perform the behaviors that align with organizational goals.

DAYDREAM BELIEVERS—
GOOGLE OFFERS 20% FREE TIME

Google is famous for giving employees free time to brainstorm their own creative ideas. In fact, 20% of a Google employee's workday is his to do with as he pleases. That's a whole day a week! Employees can use the time however they want: They can go to yoga class, take a walk around campus, or even simply sit at their desks and daydream. Google's philosophy is that giving employees leeway when it comes to their workdays ultimately leads to innovation.

Google's "20 Percent Time" perk has paid off over the years. In 2008, for example, Google employee Alec Proudfoot used his free time to dream up the RechargeIT project, which retrofitted standard hybrid cars into more efficient hybrid cars that could be recharged electrically overnight, with the goal of accelerating the adoption of plug-in electric vehicle technology. At the time, no commercially available plug-in hybrid electric vehicles were on the market, so Proudfoot's project was ahead of its time. There are now several companies manufacturing electric vehicles, and Google has retired the project, but they still use a fleet of Proudfoot's prototype cars, now under the name Gfleet, at Google headquarters in Mountain View, California.[8]

AdWords and AdSense, two massive moneymaking products, also came directly out of the 20 Percent Time incentive. They account for more than a quarter of Google's $50 billion 2012 revenue!

Google's program has been so successful that other tech giants have followed its lead. In 2012, for instance, Apple announced its aptly named Blue Sky initiative, encouraging employees to spend one-fifth of their time on pet projects.[9]

Nik Wallenda has taught us that in order to achieve balance, you need three legs on your data stool. When it comes to creating incentives, using empirical data in addition to academic and anecdotal data can mean the difference between strong and steady incentives that align with goals and behavior, and those that can't stand up.

Sales leaders are almost singularly focused on increasing motivation through compensation; finance folks, on the other hand, are concerned with such details as accuracy, analytics, stability, and predictability. Can the needs of Sales and Finance be satisfied *at the same time*? Yes, they can, and I'll show you in chapter five how organizations can use data to accomplish the tall task of satisfying the needs of both.

Visit www.GameThePlan.com to watch videos that share how to apply this chapter's principles in your own company.

CHAPTER 5

SALES VS. FINANCE: WE *CAN* GET ALONG!

Sales and finance departments have historically had a tension-filled relationship, seemingly always at odds with each other. Getting them to get along can seem like one of the biggest barriers to reaching organizational goals. Sales leaders are known for doing anything—*anything*—to increase sales, including using spendy gamification strategies and potentially bank-breaking tactics—think promising large bonuses and sending reps on expensive trips—to get the competitive juices flowing. Finance folks are known for putting the kibosh on these tactics in an effort to control spending. Finance execs complain that tactics to increase sales are too risky or too expensive, while sales leaders complain that tactics to rein in spending don't allow them to maximize potential.

But despite this friction, Sales and Finance actually want the same thing: for the business to grow, to reach its goals, and to be successful.

In a way, Sales and Finance are a lot like the professional tennis players Venus and Serena Williams. The sisters have played dozens of competitive matches against each other, some of which were Grand Slam singles finals. They both want, and play, to win, but

SOLVE THE TAKE-THE-BONUS-AND-RUN SYNDROME— THREE WAYS TO RETAIN YOUR ROCK STARS

Sometimes, what seems like an inspiring incentive plan can backfire and make you lose your top performers.

Motivational speaker and consultant Barry Maher told me about one company he worked with that offered impressive bonuses—up to 40% of compensation—and paid them out just once a year, in March. As you might imagine, this incentive structure attracted some serious talent. But the company started to notice another undesirable trend: "People who had been thinking of leaving the company, and particularly the best people, all gave their notice in April," Barry said. Each spring, the company found itself scrambling to replace its top performers.

"Thirty case studies taken from the 11 most relevant research papers on the costs of employee turnover demonstrate that it costs businesses about *one-fifth of a worker's salary* to replace that worker."
—Center for American Progress[1]

Said simply, it's costly to replace your top performers regularly. Here are three ways to retain your rock stars:

1. **Identify turnover spikes.** Look at your human resources data. (For more information on how to get the most out of your HR data, see chapter nine.) If you notice, for instance, that a bonus payout is often followed by resignations en masse, it might be time to rethink your bonus schedule.

2. **Use data to check in with top performers at key times.** When performance numbers start to slip and there's no economic or company-wide reason for the downturn, it might be a sign that your employees are losing interest. It's time to reengage them with more creative goals and rewards.

3. **Introduce timely incentives.** Counter periodic performance lags with surprise gestures of appreciation. For example, take your team out to lunch or offer a one-time SPIF.

Time to turn down the turnover.

each has a different approach for getting the job done. Venus is more thoughtful and tactical; Serena exhibits a more aggressive, high-risk style of play.

For the few hours the Williams sisters are on the court battling it out against each other, they are divided. But once the point is played and one of them wins, the losing sister is gracious, joining the throng in cheering for the winning sister in her remaining matches. They are family, after all.

Just like the Williams sisters, Sales and Finance have their battles, but ultimately they are family, united in the same goals. The friction between them, if managed correctly, can only help the teams become better—separate and together.

In this chapter, I'll explore the needs and desires of each department, common conflicts between them, and how we can resolve those conflicts so we can all feel a bit more love.

THINGS SALESPEOPLE LIKE

With their primary focus on maximizing sales, sales leaders are inherently fixated on attraction, engagement, retention, and sales performance.

Top Talent

Sales leaders want rock star reps. You know, the ones who hit it out of the park and meet or exceed quota month after month? The thing is, their competitors want these super-salespeople too. So how do sales leaders attract the best?

It's pretty simple. They do what they need to do to make top talent *want* to work for them.

A couple of years ago, a mustachioed product marketer named Matthew Epstein produced a well-known YouTube video in which he asked Google to hire him.[2] Google had built a reputation of being so cool they no longer had to seek out top talent. Top talent came looking for *them*.

Companies don't have to be as cool as Google to have great people vying for their attention, but they do have to make an effort if they want to compete with industry leaders. Sales leaders who understand what attracts and motivates top performers are constantly pushing for these two key things:

Low Turnover: Most sales leaders cringe at the thought of their top reps going to competitors. As a matter of fact, the thought is so unpalatable that many are willing to do whatever it takes to get their best employees to stick around. But when all is said and done, the things that emotionally tie a rep to the organization are the same things that attract that rep in the first place. Reps want a terrific company culture, competitive salary, and benefits. They also look for onboarding, coaching, and training tactics that give them a better chance of succeeding.

Maximum Productivity: The ultimate goal of every sales leader is to see his or her team consistently close deals. To that end, sales leaders seek creative, flexible compensation plans capable of motivating different groups and subsets of employees. They want plans that work in the moment, but they also want to be able to modify plans if internal or external events require a shift. Likewise, they recognize that even the most engaged and motivated reps can't increase output and secure maximum productivity without the right support, so they seek to introduce the onboarding, training, and coaching programs that rock star reps are looking for to help them succeed.

THINGS FINANCE PEOPLE LIKE

A 2011 report conducted by staffing company Robert Half indicates that Sales and Finance have plenty in common. According to the study, which polled 1,400 CFOs from a random sample of U.S. companies with twenty or more employees, staff morale and motivation are among the top three challenges faced by today's financial leaders.[3]

Also making the list of top three challenges were improving profitability and controlling spending. Finance's primary concerns include:

Cash Flow Management: The strategic planners of your business, finance leaders are tasked with defining and measuring cash flow, and then using what they learn to decide how the organization distributes capital. They must make sure that the amount of dollars invested in sales compensation and the amount of dollars earned in revenue are balanced in their favor. It makes sense that finance leaders don't want to hear things like "I know this SPIF is expensive, but it will work in the long run . . . trust me!" or "Don't think of this incentive as a bank-breaker, think of it as an investment!" Finance leaders deal in cold, hard realities, and they want proof, not promises.

NON-CASH REWARDS WITH NO CASH OUTLAY

Non-cash rewards can be as simple or as extravagant as you like. Here are a few with no direct cost.

- Common stock option
- An extra day off of the employee's choosing
- Use of a conference room for a 30-minute catnap
- Use of the boss's vacation home for a weekend (without the boss)
- A paid day off to volunteer

Minimizing Risk: Finance leaders want to know exactly how changes to compensation plans and sales organization structure will affect the bottom line. Also, more than a decade after the passing of the Sarbanes-Oxley (SOX) Act of 2002, a law designed to protect investors from fraudulent accounting practices by corporations, finance leaders want to mitigate major financial and legal exposure. To adhere to SOX, they must be able to demonstrate that all incentive compensation paid complies with the compensation plan, that no undisclosed side agreements were in effect, and that compensation calculations are valid and correct.

Managing Growth: When your business grows, it usually means you've done something right. But balancing that growth with resources can be tricky for finance leaders. Finance leaders want to make sure they have the resources they need to meet customer demand and to keep things moving in the right direction, but they also want to make sure that expenses associated with growth don't outstrip revenue.

HURRYING IN THE HURRICANE

Sometimes, circumstances beyond your company's control will force you to make compensation decisions outside of your normal strategy. Here's how three companies responded when natural disasters rendered their normal compensation strategies ineffective and inappropriate

1. Uber Listened to Its Head, Not Its Heart

Uber, a thoroughly modern car service that competes with standard cab companies in several cities around the U.S., lets users order rides through a smartphone app. During Hurricane Sandy in 2012, when the New York City subway system closed temporarily, Uber experienced a surge in its business—unstoppable New Yorkers were determined to get around despite the superstorm. In order to motivate more of its self-employed drivers to get on the road, Uber instituted what it called "surge pricing," a tactic that doubles the price of the service for riders in order to pay the drivers higher commissions.

B. A. Brooklyn
@B_A_Brooklyn

🐦 **Follow**

Hey @uber_nyc I love you but doubling the price for "intense demand" when there's no transit/disaster sounds like price gouging to me.

7:11 AM - 31 Oct 2012

While Uber thought the move made good business sense, because riders wouldn't have to wait for cars and drivers would work in the storm for higher pay, the company's customer base was not amused and took to Twitter to voice complaints.

Uber quickly recognized that getting more drivers out on the road was crucial, but it was equally important that its good reputation remain intact. So the company normalized the pricing, yet continued to pay the drivers double until Hurricane Sandy was over. This cost Uber more in dollars, of course, but it paid off in public relations and mitigated the Twitter backlash.

2. Sprint Acted Fast to Support Its Team

In 2005, Hurricane Katrina left millions of people without cell service in the South and obliterated some Sprint stores, leaving employees with literally no workplace. Sprint worked hard to restore service for its customers, and at the same time, it made sure the disaster didn't stop its in-store reps' paychecks. Even though reps couldn't make their usual sales to gain commissions, Sprint quickly announced a special SPIF to reward team member loyalty and patience until business was up and running again.

3. Incentivizing for Salty Snack Sales

Whereas the wallets of some industries are hit hard by hurricanes, the salty snacks business booms when clouds roll in. Customers love to stockpile foods like chips when a disaster is imminent, so when a hurricane was looming, one snack company decided to overstock store shelves ahead of time to maximize its profit. But it ran into a problem: Its delivery drivers were on salary and didn't have a lot of motivation to hustle. To inspire drivers, the snack company paid double compensation in the days leading up to the storm. The drivers rallied, and customers were at least guaranteed the comfort of salty snacks in a time of crisis.

Inevitably, natural disasters happen. Having an emergency compensation plan in place before a hurricane or other calamity can make the difference in your team's morale and the public's perception of your product—and enable you to give back to your community in a time of need.

WHERE IS THE LOVE?

While Sales and Finance are united in the big goal of boosting productivity and growing the business, their specific needs continue to divide them. How many of the five common "wars" waged between these two key departments, described on the following pages, sound familiar to you?

The Cost Clash

Both Sales and Finance are concerned with compensation cost of sales (CCOS), but for slightly different reasons. Sales leaders want an answer to the question, "How much do we need to spend to attract, motivate, and retain reps?" Finance leaders want an answer to the question, "Out of every dollar we earn in revenue, how much are we spending on base and incentive?"

Finance considers CCOS a key metric for making strategic decisions, but the average sales leader probably can't tell you how many checks are cut for one deal, how payment is determined, whether everyone receiving a check contributes to the sale, and whether commissions complement the level of contribution. Sales leaders use incentive compensation to drive action and increase performance. Finance leaders also want to use incentive compensation to drive action and increase performance, but they want to know *exactly* how much they're spending—and where—in order to do so.

Both teams know that breakdowns and failures occur when there's an imbalance between money coming in and money going out. But sales leaders are driven by a killer instinct to close as many sales deals as possible, while finance leaders are driven by an equally ambitious instinct to mitigate risk. Finance may view Sales as a group of reckless cowboys who increase organizational risk, while Sales may view Finance as the sheriffs who handcuff them and disable them from rounding up the maximum number of cattle.

The Spending Skirmish

Sales leaders want to spend more on sales because they view expenditures as an investment. Finance is constantly pushing back, trying to reduce costs and questioning every SPIF, bonus, training, coaching session, and expense account.

So, who's right?

Both Sales and Finance have good arguments. Should you always be thinking about reducing costs, like finance people do? The right answer is *yes*. At the same time, however, you should be spending *more* on sales. Spending more increases profits and revenue. But how do you reduce spending while spending more? Aha! No wonder Sales and Finance have such a contentious relationship!

To solve this riddle, the two departments both need to shift their focus a bit. Finance needs to think less about saving and more about *where* they can spend to see the best results. Likewise, Sales needs to think a bit more about *where* to spend instead of how much to spend. This may mean spending less in one area so the sales leaders can spend more in another. For example, if territory optimization could use a cash injection, they may need to do more homework and figure out if they should increase sales spending in certain territories instead of just across the board.

Of course, getting Sales and Finance to meet in the middle here is easier said than done. Finance needs to be convinced that spending more makes good sense; Sales must stop considering across-the-board spending an investment. Instead, they must be a bit more thoughtful about where to allocate dollars.

The Caps Conflict

Finance folks like to put caps on rewards, claiming that caps prevent sales reps from "gaming the plan," or engaging in unacceptable behavior that puts the organization at risk or breaks the bank. They feel better knowing exactly how much a rep stands to make if he maxes out. Finance people always have good intentions when they cap an incentive compensation plan. They don't want excessive commissions to end up costing more than the sale itself.

But caps drive sales leaders crazy, and for good reason. Salespeople know that caps encourage reps to relax after goals are met, which makes it difficult for those reps to reach their maximum potential. It's human nature. If you're given a reward for jumping a certain height, why would you make an effort to jump any higher? (For more information on why we think capping commission belongs in the Dirty Dozen of incentive compensation mistakes, see chapter three.)

As difficult as it is, finance leaders need to let go of caps and let reps reach as high as they can, reminding themselves that as a salesperson's commission rises, so too does the organization's revenue. But in order to do this, plans must be structured so that the benefit of going beyond quota always exceeds the cost. If the plan isn't working this way, reps shouldn't be punished. Instead, Sales and Finance should work together to fix the plan.

The Flexibility Fight

Finance people like predictable incentive compensation plans that have already been proven. Once they have a good thing going, they are loath to mess with it. Unfortunately, rigid compensation plans fail to take into account internal and external changes, such as those in sales roles, rep demographic, competition, and the marketplace. What worked well a couple of years ago—even a couple of months ago—may not work now.

Sales leaders, on the other hand, are all about flexibility. They just learned about new gamification strategies at a sales conference, and they want to try them out *pronto*! No matter that the current plan isn't broken, or that a sales force largely comprising Baby Boomers most likely will not respond to such strategies. It's new, it's exciting, all the cool kids are doing it . . . let's give it a whirl!

How do you resolve this issue? Finance types are much more likely to embrace more flexible incentive compensation plans if they have a clear picture of which incentives are working and which are not, as well as a strong read on internal and external changes. It's not that they are resistant to change; it's that they want a reason for the change and some proof that it has a good chance of working.

Sales folks, for their part, need to respect Finance's need for realities and projections. The best way to do this is to consider changes to the incentive plan thoughtfully and back them up with evidence that proves changes will help get the most out of the sales strategy.

The Training Tussle

According to the American Society of Training and Development's 2012 state of the industry report, American businesses spent a whopping $156.2 billion on employee training in 2011.[4] There's no doubt, coaching and training are hot.

Salespeople advocate training and coaching because both means of professional development increase the odds of sales rep success. Not only does this improve the organization's bottom line, but it also attracts and retains top talent.

If you ask Finance, they probably have a good idea of how much they spend on training per salesperson. But what they don't have is a good handle on ROI, which leads them to ask, "Is it really worth it?" If sales leaders are taking a one-size-fits-all approach, the answer may be *no*.

Sales leaders can increase Finance's buy-in by determining the effectiveness of coaching and training, by identifying the sales reps who could most benefit from training, and by customizing training and coaching programs to increase performance where it's needed most.

CONNECTION PERFECTION: THREE WAYS TO TIGHTEN TIES BETWEEN SALES AND FINANCE

Sales and Finance might never completely see eye to eye. We can't change the fact that they come from different corners of the business, or that their specific needs conflict more often than not. What we can do, though, is give each team the tools they need to meet in the middle and inspire confidence in the other, so conflicts and issues don't continue to obstruct the organization's forward momentum. Instead of working against each other, Sales and Finance can work together toward the common goal of building the best business possible.

Good Planning: Agreeing to Accelerate Sales Through Predictive Modeling

You can satisfy Finance's need for accuracy, analytics, predictability, and stability, while also satisfying Sales' need for motivation and flexibility, by agreeing to accelerate sales and using predictive modeling to show what will happen.

The historical data in your incentive compensation management software can:

- Check your quotas to determine whether they are too high or too low. Use the information to set high (yet still attainable) quotas, remove commission caps, and structure your plan so the benefit of going beyond quota exceeds the cost.

- Consider past and current sales roles, customer needs, competition, and the economy so you can develop an incentive compensation plan that aligns with these areas.

- Enable you to drill into your territories, products, and performers and create "what if" scenarios that help you determine where to increase spending for long-term improvements.

- Help you determine exactly where to allocate funds for training and coaching.

- Determine where quota attainment drop-offs occur, and then adjust them to send a signal to reps that encourages them to maximize selling potential.

- Help you adjust quota timing, so that more reps reach 80 percent or more of quota. Xactly's data set shows that in companies with an annual quota, only 60 percent of sales reps go over 80 percent of quota. Companies with a quarterly quota, on the other hand, saw a 7 percent increase!

- Know exactly how much your organization spends on sales compensation, how many people are paid per deal, and whether every person sharing credit deserves it.

- Split your predictive model into three buckets of attainment when forecasting costs: reps who don't hit their numbers, reps who hit between 80 percent and 120 percent of quota, and reps who go above 120 percent. Once you put a lot of leverage into the plan, you will be able to adjust as revenues increase.

When you use the historical data in your incentive compensation software for predictive modeling, the sales team gets its accelerators and can freely encourage its reps to blow through the numbers. The finance team doesn't have to worry about breaking the bank because the data forecasts exactly what will happen. Everyone's happy.

Create Killer Calculations and Formulas

Effective compensation design depends upon accurate, accessible calculations and formulas that not only determine optimal pay levels, incentives, and bonuses but also determine the correct *mix* of each of these components. An effective compensation plan must be flexible enough to adjust to internal and external changes, and the reps must easily understand the plan in order for it to drive desired behaviors.

Formulas and calculations that are entered by hand into spreadsheets are prone to error. Incentive compensation software, on the other hand, imports accurate numbers. This real-time data empowers Sales to build strong, effective incentive compensation plans that can be tested and adjusted. Best of all, finance leaders are on board with these plans because they believe in the calculations and formulas.

Verify and Measure

Whether you're trying to achieve revenue, profit, market share, customer satisfaction, new account acquisition, or account/revenue retention, the data from your incentive compensation software can help you measure your performance. This allows Sales to make adjustments based on the data and Finance to have faith in those adjustments because the proof is easy to find, track, and analyze. In addition to ensuring that spending is on track, automated incentive compensation tools verify, measure, and guarantee consistency between commission plans and information used to calculate and report on commissions, ensuring that your organization remains compliant.

———

Sales leaders want to do whatever possible to increase sales, while finance leaders focus on controlling spending. With the right strategy, both sides can find harmony and put the focus on what they have in common, not on what they don't. When these two essential departments work together toward the common goal of increasing sales, the key ingredient is motivation. In the next chapter, I'll help you understand and tap into the science of motivation so you can really begin to craft a plan that inspires performance.

Visit www.GameThePlan.com to watch videos that share how
to apply this chapter's principles in your own company.

CHAPTER 6

THE DARK ART OF MOTIVATION

Remember back in the day when all you had to do to motivate your sales team was threaten their survival?

Okay, me neither. But sales motivation used to be a lot simpler because people were primarily concerned with finding food and shelter. The basic need to survive meant that the average caveman wasn't going to let others pick up the slack while he chilled with a pint of Ben & Jerry's in front of Netflix. Let's face it: If he missed the opportunity to kill and eat that pygmy hippo, there was a good chance that he and his family wouldn't live to see another day.

Thanks to evolution, food and shelter are much easier to come by. The survival of a typical sales rep is not threatened on a daily basis, and she's no longer motivated solely by fear of dying. Our needs and desires have evolved, and so too have the things that drive us.

Today's sales reps don't want to simply survive. They want to *succeed*. Yet many organizations still go the caveman route, failing to more deeply consider human behavior and desires when developing their incentive compensation plans. They apply a single definition of "success," failing to realize that success looks different to unique individuals, groups, and generations. Or they develop across-the-board reward and punishment systems, and then wonder why all employees don't respond in the desired ways.

Companies succeed in direct parallel to how they incentivize their employees. The good news is that when it comes to human motivation, we have lots of science on our side. When you understand the science of motivation, you position yourself to understand what makes employees tick. And when you understand what makes your employees tick, you position yourself to win.

In this chapter, I'll debunk some common myths about motivation as a "dark art" and explore, instead, the science that drives the concept. Finally, I'll show you how to tap into your team's psychology to inspire performance.

BUT FIRST, A FEW MYTH-UNDERSTANDINGS ABOUT MOTIVATION

To inspire and incent your team, you must first recognize and acknowledge common misconceptions you and others in your organization might hold about motivation.

Myth-understanding #1: Having a job should be motivation enough.

During a recession this might be true, but failing to incent employees because the unemployment rate is high and jobs are scarce is shortsighted. According to the Job Openings and Labor Turnover Survey conducted by the U.S. Department of Labor and released in July 2013, the number of "quits"—voluntary separations initiated by employees—rose 42 percent from the postrecession trough

HOW MUCH CAN STRESSED-OUT EMPLOYEES COST YOU?

A 1992 United Nations report titled "Job Stress: The 20th Century Disease" says organizations aren't doing enough to help employees cope with stress.[1] No doubt, job-related stress has skyrocketed. According to a survey conducted by Northwestern National Life, 40% of workers report that their job is "very or extremely stressful."[2]

When a person feels stress, a signal is sent to the brain to prepare the body to defend itself. Hormones are released to sharpen senses, deepen respiration, quicken the pulse, and tense muscles. This "fight or flight" response comes in very handy in emergency situations, but it can be detrimental to your health when experienced constantly as a result of unresolved stressful situations. Ultimately, being on constant alert fatigues the body and the mind, and the body becomes less effective at defending itself.

Many organizations don't realize the cost of having (much less contributing to) stressed-out employees in their place of business. Consider these long-term effects of workplace stress:

- Medical Costs. According to the *Journal of Occupational and Environmental Medicine*, health care costs are almost 50% greater for workers who report high levels of stress.[3]

- Diminished Productivity. According to a study published by the American Psychological Association in 2009, 51% of employees said they were less productive at work because of stress.[4]

- Employee Turnover. Research conducted by the American Psychological Association in 2007 shows that 52% of employees have looked for a new job, declined a promotion, or left a job because of workplace stress.[5]

- Absenteeism. According to a report released by the U.S. Bureau of Labor Statistics in 2001, the median number of days that employees were absent from work as a result of stress and anxiety was 25. This figure was more than four times the median number of days for nonfatal injuries and illnesses.[6]

in 2009 to 2.1 million in May 2013.[7] Organizations that don't keep up with incentives during times when they have the upper hand can face dissatisfied employees and an exodus of top talent when a shift in the job market occurs.

Myth-understanding #2: Money is the greatest motivator.

While money is important to employees and plays a large part in attracting and retaining top talent, leaders often make the mistake of thinking that money is a motivational cure-all. But the truth is, throwing more coin at underperforming sales reps might not get them to change their behavior. Or even worse, it can result in nega-

THE FIVE BIGGEST MOTIVATION MISTAKES

When it comes to motivating employees, you can learn from the mistakes of others. Here are the top five mistakes we see in compensation strategies and practices:

1. **Inappropriate ranking of reps.** When a team leader subjectively ranks his reps according to his impression of their performance, it's called favoritism. A better tactic? Measuring their actual output. But beware of ranking your reps strictly on numbers. What if most of your reps are selling in the low hundred thousands, but two of your reps are neck and neck at $1 million and $999,999? Does it really make sense to label the latter rep "number two"? Considering that both reps are killing it, perhaps it's a better motivator to place them in a tie for number one.

2. **Using compensation to drive adoption of customer relationship management.** CRM failures result in loss of time and money, business disruption, and upset customers. One of the biggest pitfalls in this critical business aspect is lack of supervisor involvement. Instead of using comp to drive

CRM adoption, it's important that executives and supervisors make sure people are ready and processes are in place. If your people aren't ready and your processes aren't defined, CRM technology won't fix those things—it will only make unmotivated behaviors more obvious.

3. **Ignoring how motivating one team for higher performance impacts another.** Some manufacturers focus closely on maximizing their factory productivity and minimizing variances for optimal output, but then they ignore the impact that production has on distribution. If you're making a million cupcakes, great, but if they're not moving through your channels before they spoil, what's the point? The process needs to be considered from beginning to end.

4. **Over-incentivizing for a particular behavior.** Leaders we talked to at one company noticed that when their reps visited prospects on-site, close rates went up. So they created a SPIF encouraging this behavior. Soon after, they saw that reps were visiting every site, but mysteriously, the close rates were spiraling downward. Why? Reps were visiting weak prospects as well as strong ones because they knew they'd get bonuses regardless of the meeting's outcome. So, the company changed the SPIF: Instead of providing a flat bonus, leaders empowered reps to offer prospects discounts during a site visit. As a result, the close rates spiked.

5. **Motivating one rep to mimic another's winning techniques.** A lot of companies operate with the mistaken impression that if a certain style and behavior works for Rep A, it will work for Rep B, C, and so on. But sales reps have different approaches; a behavior that works for one rep might not work for another. Let each rep find his or her own style.

tive behaviors. Van Gogh, one of the world's most brilliant artists, didn't let his penniless state stop him from creating masterpieces. In contrast, financier–Ponzi schemer Bernie Madoff was clearly motivated only by money, and look where that got him.

TIME IS CURRENCY

Money is a valuable commodity, but so is time. In the United States, we're conditioned to believe in the nine-to-five workday. So if we score a shorter day while making the same amount of money that we would earn in eight hours, we think we're getting off easy.

UPS and FedEx take advantage of this perception by motivating their drivers with the possibility of more free time. Drivers are given a set daily route they must complete, but once they finish that route, they are done for the day. If a driver figures out a way to manage his route more efficiently (while always driving safely, of course!), he works shorter days, amassing more time off.

This strategy gives drivers both a sense of responsibility and the perception of freedom. And it lends UPS and FedEx a reputation for quick, reliable service—which sells.

Studies support my belief that money is not a top motivator. A 2012 survey conducted by Galaxy Research asked 1,277 workers what drove them to work harder. Only 20 percent of respondents said money and bonuses.[8] The rest were divided, citing support of colleagues, workplace culture, growth opportunities, and recognition as main motivators.

Myth-understanding #3: Nothing lights a fire like fear.

Fear isn't a good motivator; it's a *great* motivator. Just ask anyone who has ever been fearful of losing her job or livelihood.

But it's only great in the short term.

When fear is used to motivate, employees usually kick it up a notch, at least *temporarily*. A low-performing sales rep may even be scared into meeting his monthly quota. But motivation by fear never produces lasting results. Instead, it creates a stressful, unhealthy environment—one that good employees will leave as soon as the opportunity arises.

As we learned in chapter three, a well-done compensation plan increases employee engagement first, then happiness. Employers with happier, less-stressed-out employees can expect lower absenteeism, employee turnover, and medical costs, as well as higher productivity.

Myth-understanding #4: Good motivation theories and practices will work for all employees.

There are, quite simply, no universally applicable rules for motivating people. Plenty of studies have been published comparing motives of different occupational groups and "types" of personalities (think Myers-Briggs), but not enough emphasis has been placed on the need for individual motivation.

Many organizational leaders accept that what motivates research and development teams, for example, might not motivate sales teams. They may even design different compensation plans for these groups. But that's where the differentiation stops. They fail to recognize that motives vary widely among individuals, even among people with similar occupations, in the same department, on the same team, or with the same personality profiles. Sales leaders who trot out one-size-fits-all incentive plans don't know how to respond when some reps consistently meet and exceed quota while others limp along. An easy way out of this dilemma is not to buy into the next myth.

Myth-understanding #5: Sales reps are either naturally motivated or they're not.

Artistic ability and athletic ability can be developed and improved, but it's generally accepted that some people have more raw talent in these areas than others. Thinking that some people are more inherently motivated than others is one of the most dangerous misunderstandings of all. Sales leaders who label reps as either fundamentally "lazy" or "go-getters" fail to get the most out of individuals in both of those groups.

We've all been on teams where some people thrive on challenges, pushing themselves to achieve, while others don't seem interested in engaging in those same challenges. Time-strapped management may not spend precious hours or a lot of effort motivating the former group, thinking they'll get along fine on their own. But at some point, your best employees may become bored, frustrated, or disengaged simply because you're not paying attention to their changing needs.

On the other end of the spectrum, leaders occasionally write poor performers off as unmotivated. No doubt, sometimes an individual simply doesn't have the chops to be a sales rep and should be dismissed. That being said, everyone is motivated by *something*. Even the rep you catch playing video games during work hours has some motivation behind his or her actions. If you don't learn what that something is and figure out how to direct it toward work, you could miss out on a highly productive employee.

MOWING LAWNS FOR MOOLA

Many company leaders think incentive compensation pertains to sales and only sales. But anyone can be motivated to work harder—and get creative—with the right incentive.

One of our VPs of sales at Xactly remembers his first job working for a landscaping company, mowing lawns every day during the summer. He was paid by the lawn cut, not by the hour, so he enlisted a friend to work with him. Together they created a system for mowing a lot of lawns quickly, which resulted in more cash in their pockets. Our VP-to-be's lifelong passion for winning in business was born!

You might not think of manual labor as a category that can be affected by compensation strategies, but think again. It's human nature to respond to any challenge that promises payoff, so get creative with your incentive strategy and you'll see your employees get creative about winning.

THE BIRTH OF THE CARROT . . . AND THE STICK

Quite a few organizations use the popular default principle of the carrot and the stick to drive motivation. This simple system rewards desirable behaviors (the carrot) and punishes detrimental behaviors (the stick). But while it's one of the most widely used methods out there, it's probably not all it's cracked up to be.

The carrot principle began to grow legs as a management theory in the late 1800s, when the son of a prominent Philadelphia family, Frederick Winslow Taylor, scored an apprenticeship at Midvale Steel and began to develop ideas that would form the foundation of scientific management. Taylor, whose main goal was to improve industrial productivity and efficiency, strongly believed there was one best way to do things—whether you were building cars or playing tennis.[9]

(As an interesting aside, Taylor won the United States Lawn Tennis Association Doubles Championship in 1881.[10])

In 1911, Taylor published his book, *The Principles of Scientific Management*, which tells organizations how to get consistent results out of their workforces.[11] At the heart of scientific management was the idea that tasks must be approached in a scientific manner—for example, measuring the order in which people did tasks, how they moved, the environment they worked in, and the equipment they used—to increase productivity, improve performance, and result in a happier workforce. Taylor outlined a system in which management specified a task, detailed exactly how that task was to be done, and allotted an exact time for completing it. If a workman succeeded in doing the task correctly within the allotted time frame, Taylor suggested he receive a bonus of 30 percent to 100 percent of his regular wages.[12]

Scientific Management and the Pig Iron Gang

In chapter two of his book, Taylor tells the reader how the introduction of scientific management improved the performance of Bethlehem Steel's pig iron gang, which comprised seventy-five men. Each man on the gang picked up a piece of pig iron weighing about ninety-two pounds, walked it up an inclined plank leading into a railroad car, and dropped it into the car. At the end of the day, each man loaded, on average, about twelve and a half tons of pig iron.

But when Taylor and his group studied the task, they estimated that each man should load, on average, forty-seven to forty-eight tons of pig iron per day—almost *four times* the amount they were currently loading. Taylor's goal, then, was to not only motivate a significant increase in the amount of pig iron loaded per day, without also inspiring the men to strike, but also to bring about contentment in the workforce, even though the men would be doing significantly more work.

First, Taylor carefully selected workmen who were strong enough to physically handle loading forty-seven tons of pig iron per day. After identifying four men, Taylor settled on a man he named "Schmidt" in his book to be his test subject. Schmidt, who was then earning $1.15 per day, was known for placing a high value on money. He had saved enough money to buy a plot of land, and he was building himself a house during his off hours.

Schmidt was offered $1.85 per day if he would load pig iron according to the directions his manager gave him—pick up the pig iron, walk, and rest exactly when he was told to—without any questioning. At the end of the first day, he had loaded more than forty-seven tons of pig iron into the car and had earned $1.85—60 percent more than he had earned previously. One by one, additional men were picked out to load pig iron under the rules of scientific management.

Though Taylor's theory of scientific management certainly dealt with many layers and is more complicated than simple pay for performance, it nevertheless advanced the idea that you could significantly change behavior—and productivity as a result—simply by dangling a very big carrot.

When All Else Fails, Stick It to 'Em

In situations where the carrot doesn't work, organizations have another tool up their sleeves: the stick.

Most of us grow up with the stick principle; it was a familiar part of our everyday lives: *Clean up your room, or else!* And it worked. So it's no surprise that the principle is also used in the workplace: *Meet your quota, or else . . . you'll be terminated.*

Many of today's organizations still use the carrot and stick approach to drive motivation. But research shows that it may not be the best way to get the most out of people. While a 60 percent increase in pay was enough to get manual laborers to haul more pig iron in the early 1900s, the needs and motivations of today's workforce are much more complicated.

A meta-analysis conducted by authors associated with several different universities reviewed ninety-two quantitative studies conducted over a 120-year period to look at the link between pay and job satisfaction.[13] The study showed there was less than a 2 percent overlap between salary and job satisfaction levels, which indicates that if you want an engaged workforce, a sweet carrot composed solely of money is not the answer.

But neither is the stick. Employees who feel that they will be punished for poor performance might comply right now, but they probably won't commit for the long haul.

THE SCIENCE OF MOTIVATION: WHY DO PEOPLE DO WHAT THEY DO?

Behavioral economist Dan Ariely and career analyst and author Daniel Pink have made us think a bit more about the science behind motivation, testing long-held beliefs that people are principally motivated by money.

In a study he conducted at Harvard University, Ariely asked participants to build figures from the Lego Bionicles series. The participants were paid two dollars for the first Bionicle they built, but decreasing amounts for each subsequent Bionicle they completed.

Participants were divided into two groups. Both groups were told the Bionicles would be disassembled. In one group, built Bionicles were stored on the table in front of the test subject during the experiment and disassembled at the end. Participants in this group made eleven Bionicles, on average, before deciding it just wasn't worth the money anymore.

In the other group, Bionicles were destroyed in front of the participants as soon as they were finished. This group, on average, made only seven Bionicles before they quit.

The task was absolutely meaningless for both groups. But the results showed that seeing your handiwork—even if it was for a short time—improved your performance.[14]

In a TED Talk filmed in October 2012, Ariely says we simplify the reasons why people work, treating them like rats in a maze. We erroneously believe that as soon as we introduce money, employees are happy, and they will do whatever is asked of them.[15]

The real truth is much more complex, according to Ariely. Think about mountaineering, he says. Books about mountaineering are not filled with joy and happiness. They are filled with hardship, physical exhaustion, hunger, and frostbite. Yet people who make it to the top of a mountain and come down immediately start planning another trek up. This, he says, shows us what we care about: reaching the end. We care about the fight and the challenge. We care about accomplishing simply for the sake of accomplishing. So the types of motivational tactics that worked during the industrial age, where motivation and payment were more or less synonymous, do not work in today's knowledge economy, where the meaning of work outweighs the efficiency of work. Ariely asserts that today's workforce is motivated by meaning, challenges, ownership, creation, identity, and pride.[16]

In his book *Drive*, Daniel Pink explores why businesses fall short when focusing primarily on external motivators such as money. Using four decades of scientific research, he concludes that the intrinsic rewards of autonomy, mastery, and purpose are where it's at in today's workforce. Employers can tap into the intrinsic motivator of autonomy by giving employees choices as to how to control various aspects of their jobs, while the motivator of mastery can be found in challenging employees to reach their fullest potential. (For more about how challenges engage employees and make them happier, read about stretch goals in chapter three.) Employers can use the intrinsic motivator of purpose by connecting employees to things that are larger than themselves, that is, by showing them how their work impacts the organization, a particular group of people, or even the world.

FIVE CRITICAL ELEMENTS: TAP INTO YOUR TEAM'S PSYCHOLOGY AND INSPIRE PERFORMANCE

Ultimately, motivations are highly personal and individual. What motivates one person might not motivate another. While an organization's incentive compensation strategy must take the individual into account, the science of motivation tells us that the five elements described in the list that follows should always be considered:

1. **Meaning**

   Harvard Business School professor Teresa Amabile and independent researcher Steven Kramer, authors of *The Progress Principle*, collected almost twelve thousand electronic diary entries from 238 employees in seven different companies to find out why employee engagement was on the downturn. They found that of all the factors that resulted in employee engagement, the most important was making progress in meaningful work.

   Leaders can inject meaning into employees' work by finding out what really matters to each and every one of them. Then, they can inject what matters into the work environment by:

THE REAL GENESIS OF FREE TIME:
EVER HEARD OF THE POST-IT NOTE?

Though Google often gets innovator's credit for offering employees a 20 Percent Time incentive (see details in the sidebar titled "Daydream Believers—Google Offers 20% Free Time" in chapter four), 3M originated the free time idea in the 1970s. (It makes over 50,000 products, which run the gamut from office to medical supplies.) In fact, employee free time is directly responsible for one of my favorite inventions ever: the Post-it Note.

3M's free-time program, "15 Percent Time," allows employees to spend 15% of their paid work time coming up with creative ideas and inventions of their own. In 1974, Art Fry, a 3M scientist, was using his 15 Percent Time to invent the perfect bookmark—"one that kept place in his church hymnal," according to Co.DESIGN—by applying adhesive to a slip of paper. The prototype he ended up with was perfected and became a worldwide office staple

Today, 3M does more than $20 billion in annual sales and holds over 22,800 patents. Much of its success and innovation ties back to 15 Percent Time, which it still offers employees to this day Not only does 15 Percent Time yield creative results from smart employees who thrive when given space to think creatively, it also helps attract the best talent.

> **"*Play is essential*; it's through play that you find connections between things that might not be at all obvious through logic or practicality."**
> **—Jim Coudal of Signals.com**

By the way, employees like Art Fry who come up with winning ideas aren't just given a pat on the back by 3M. They're given an equity share in the resulting product.

a. Showing the connection between what those employees do and the purpose of the organization;

b. Coaching managers to provide better feedback and recognition; and

c. Empowering employees to share their ideas.

2. Recognition

In *The Carrot Principle*, authors Adrian Gostick and Chester Elton discuss a study they did of more than 200,000 employees over a ten-year period. Their research showed that employees produced the best results when they received praise or accolades. As a matter of fact, recognition yielded significantly better results than did money.

To effectively recognize employees, give them relevant, objective measures and tell them every day how they are doing. Check performance data frequently and reward top-performing reps by putting their names on a leaderboard, recognizing their good work in an email blast, or calling them in to tell them exactly how they've contributed to the overall success of the organization.

3. Autonomy/Choice

In 2006, Edward L. Deci and Richard M. Ryan, psychologists from the University of Rochester, conducted several studies to evaluate how subjects performed when they were feeling controlled as opposed to feeling self-directed. They found that the group that was allowed to act based on their own opinions persisted significantly longer in a puzzle-solving activity than did those who were told how to solve the puzzle, or who were pressured to solve it in a specific manner.[17]

Finding ways to grant employees autonomy in everyday

work will go a long way toward increasing energy, engagement, and commitment. Atlassian, an Australian software company, developed what it called the "FedEx day," a twenty-four-hour creativity blitz inspired by the FedEx motto, "When it absolutely, positively has to be there overnight." The company's leaders encourage employees to use each FedEx day to work on something of their choosing that does not fall within the duties of their day job, and to deliver their new project within twenty-four hours. This type of autonomy and freedom has resulted in massive energy and innovation: In the eighteen FedEx days the company has sponsored, more than 550 projects have been developed and more than forty-seven features or products delivered to the company's customers. FedEx days have gone viral, with companies like Hasbro, the Mayo Clinic, and even schools launching similar projects to inspire, motivate, and engage.[18]

Jeff Gunther, CEO of the software company Meddius, has provided the autonomy and freedom employees desire by developing a results-only work environment in which employees can work wherever they want to, whenever they want to, as long as they get their work done. As a result, both productivity and loyalty have risen.[19]

4. Competence

Employees who feel competent are much more likely to be engaged and enthused about their work. But while many organizations have competency programs designed to increase and use strengths, a good majority of these programs are misguided.

Tom Rath, coauthor of *How Full Is Your Bucket?*, says that in order to boost competence, you must develop competency programs that are grounded in science, not in guesswork. Conduct research at your organization to define the right competencies, and compare the data you collect to real performance metrics. If there's a correlation between the two—that is, if a relationship exists—you've found a solid competency with which to work.

5. Growth/Increased Responsibility

A study by Hay Group showed that one of the main reasons employees quit is that they aren't using their skills. Most individuals think long term about their careers, and they want to know that they are receiving the right training and coaching, followed up by the right challenges, to improve and progress through the ranks.[20]

It's important for organizations to determine support gaps and then apply the right training and coaching to appropriately expand skills and give the employee the best chances of succeeding. To ensure that employees are always challenged with stretch goals, performance data should be carefully analyzed and incentive compensation plans adjusted. With the right approach, you can develop an atmosphere in which employees are constantly growing and learning.

GAMIFY YOUR WORKFORCE

Have you ever logged into Facebook and wondered why so many of your intelligent friends are involved with silly games like FarmVille or Candy Crush Saga? Do you ever wonder why you have to drag your kids out of bed to get to school, but they'll get up at ungodly hours to play Minecraft?

Status, recognition, achievement, and reputation—all of these intrinsic rewards can be found in games. Organizations that understand the heady power of games have added "gamification" to their incentive compensation strategies.

But what is gamification, exactly? It's simple. Gamification is the practice of using game mechanics in nongame environments. Gamification in the enterprise is a growing trend. Your sales reps have fun, and the gaming process keeps them engaged and motivates them toward desirable behaviors. It's a win-win situation.

For example, let's say you want to get the most out of this year's annual sales meeting, so you create a trivia contest to make sure reps attend every session and are paying attention. Reps earn "points" each time they reach a certain level in the contest. The person with the most points at the end of the conference is publicly awarded with the latest electronic gadget.

In addition to being purely entertaining, let's consider the intrinsic rewards in this type of game:

- Competence: Players who answer questions correctly feel a sense of accomplishment.
- Growth: Progressing through levels gives players the satisfaction of improvement.
- Recognition: Players are motivated by the idea of receiving a public award as well as earning the respect of their coworkers and colleagues.

To this point, I've told you how incentive compensation works, and how the "dark art of motivation" factors into your strategies. Your ability to effectively implement these strategies will influence how you take compensation from a dark art to a science. In the next chapter, I'll show you how to use incentive compensation to build a company culture designed to communicate your vision, mission, and values to your workforce, as well as to the world.

Visit www.GameThePlan.com to watch videos that share how to apply this chapter's principles in your own company.

CHAPTER 7

COMPENSATION AND COMPANY CULTURE: INFLUENCING VISION, MISSION, AND VALUES

Since the dot-com boom in the 1990s, tech companies, particularly upstart entrepreneurial ventures, have lured employees with incentive perks above and beyond the traditional benefits of insurance, retirement plans, and vacation time. Today's organizations seem to be in a competition to entice employees with what I like to call "incidental incentives"—perks like $4,000 of "baby cash" for new parents at Facebook, on-prem volleyball courts and heated swimming pools at Google, and free eats (breakfast, lunch, dinner, and snacks) at Dropbox. But with 71 percent of today's workforce still actively disengaged on the job[1], are these perks really the key drivers of top-performing staff? No. Don't get me wrong; these perks are great in that they do play a role in attracting talent, but they aren't the key motivational drivers of your best employees.

I'd even argue that these incidental incentives don't help to build and cultivate a strong and vibrant company culture nearly as much as one might suspect.

In an article titled "The Best Workplace Luxuries Anywhere," which appeared in the August 6, 2010, edition of *Forbes* magazine, Stanford University professor Jeffrey Pfeffer, who studies workplaces, agrees with me. Pfeffer says perks are nice, but they're only useful when there's already a positive corporate culture in place that values employees.[2]

The truth is, with rare exception, motivation comes from within. No matter how competitive your salaries, no matter how amazing your benefits, no matter how many programs you design to get your people to peak performance, internal motivation doesn't happen unless employees *choose* to embrace being motivated by a company they like, believe in, and feel connected to.

Fortifying a positive culture—one that makes employees feel connected to each other and to the brand—doesn't happen as a result of serving prime beef or installing Ping-Pong tables.

True company culture comes from a workforce that's united in vision, mission, and values and is committed to executing organizational objectives. When everyone at a company is working at their peak and toward a common goal, when they feel professionally and creatively connected and have respect for each other's opinions, that's *true incentive*.

For most of us, the term *organizational culture* is familiar. But pressed to define it, what would you say?

COMPANY CULTURE, DEFINED

There's no formal definition of organizational or company culture in any dictionary. If you asked ten CEOs for the meaning, each would probably give a different definition. Most of them would agree that company culture exists, that it defines behavior and guides decisions, and that it is, therefore, important to the success of the organization. But beyond that, good luck getting them to agree on how to describe it.

To prove my point: On May 1, 2013, *Harvard Business Review*'s Michael Watkins started a discussion on LinkedIn that explored the definition of company culture.[3] More than three hundred people responded, providing their definitions, perspectives, and opinions on organizational culture. Here are a few of the definitions Watkins noted in a *Harvard Business Review* blog post two weeks later:

- "Culture is how organizations 'do things.'"

- "In large part, culture is a part of compensation."

- "Organizational culture defines a jointly shared description of an organization from within."

- "Organizational culture is the sum of values and rituals which serve as 'glue' to integrate the members of [any given] organization."

As you can see, the definitions gathered by Watkins vary widely. But, in my opinion, they are all relevant. And therein lies the challenge. In order to guide behavior and decisions, leaders must accept and understand the complexities of company culture. If leaders fail to define and understand its subtle nuances, they can't develop incentive compensation plans that drive the employee behaviors that support that culture. It's a symbiotic relationship—a strong company culture can't exist without a complementary incentive compensation plan, but a solid incentive compensation plan can't be developed without a key understanding of what you want your company culture to look like.

WHY DOES COMPANY CULTURE MATTER?

In 2001 Enron Corporation, an American energy company based out of Houston, Texas, declared bankruptcy and began a long and very public process that would eventually end in its demise. Five years later, when Enron sold off its remaining business, everyone across this country—indeed, anyone in the world with access to a television or a newspaper—was privy to what happens when an organizational culture succumbs to dysfunction.

In *Enron: The Smartest Guys in the Room*, authors Bethany McLean and Peter Elkind reveal the leader-driven malfeasance that was at the heart of the scandal. The Enron story has all the makings of a good crime novel: money laundering, gambling, fraudulent accounting practices, and even shareholder-funded trips to strip clubs. But there's no fiction in the Enron story, just fact.

For Enron, which employed twenty thousand people and was considered one of the world's industry leaders in natural gas, electricity, and other commodities, the fall from the top was particularly long. In 2000, just a year before the debacle that closed its doors, Enron claimed revenue of almost $101 billion. *Fortune* magazine had called the organization "America's Most Innovative Company" for six years in a row. To outsiders, the company had been known for its corporate responsibility and ethics.

So what happened?

Fortunately for those of us who want to learn from the mistakes of others, America's biggest Chapter 11 bankruptcy is also one of its most studied. Many of the academics, researchers, students, and business people who have dug deep into the Enron fiasco to determine how something like this happened have come to the same simple conclusion: Leaders at Enron created an organizational culture that put the bottom line ahead of doing what's right.

CAN'T GET NO (CUSTOMER) SATISFACTION

Enron wasn't the only corporate giant that lost the moral high ground. Wells Fargo has suffered its humiliations too.

Sometimes employees become focused on meeting objectives at all costs, crossing the line from gaming the plan to fraudulent practices.

If your sales reps are faking it—or, worse, engaging in fraud—their actions can land you on the front page, ruin your reputation, and engage you in a time-consuming, costly legal mess.

Take an example cited in an October 2013 article in the *Los Angeles Times*. Faced with pressures to meet sales goals, about thirty Los Angeles–region branch employees at Wells Fargo decided to seek shortcuts by opening forged accounts in customers' names.[4]

This came just two years after another Wells Fargo incentive compensation scandal made headlines. In 2011, the *Times* got hold of a series of emails that threatened workers with losses of prized perks—such as sporting event tickets—if they failed to convince customers to opt into debit overdraft protection.

Don't end up like Wells Fargo. If you want to build an incentive compensation strategy that satisfies, you must first align it with customer needs. Then, put systems in place as part of your organization's culture that blow the whistle on fraud.

In "Enron Ethics (Or: Culture Matters More Than Codes)," a paper that appeared in the July 2003 edition of the *Journal of Business Ethics*, authors Ronald R. Sims and Johannes Brinkmann describe how deeply culture, and not ethics codes—the codes that appear on a company website or in company literature—drove Enron's behavior.

According to the authors, the culture that led to Enron's downfall began unintentionally enough. When the energy industry became deregulated, Enron was able to operate outside of the lines and get creative with its products and services, using the Internet to buy and sell gas and electric power supplies to utilities, and helping these companies manage price fluctuations. Leaders were encouraged to push the limits and were rewarded for what you might call "cleverness." As ethical lines became more and more blurred, leaders bent the rules and used increasingly creative accounting processes to appear profitable to shareholders. When Jeffrey Skilling was named CEO of Enron in 2001, he developed review boards that summarily dismissed the bottom 15 percent of all employees, making it even more enticing to flirt with limits and break the rules to stay employed.

The atmosphere, as you can imagine, was brutally competitive. According to Sims and Brinkmann, as it became harder and harder to achieve additional value, rules were stretched thinner and thinner until the limits of ethical conduct were well surpassed.[5]

Corporate culture promoted and rewarded employees for unethical behavior, so it's no surprise that Enron became known for one of corporate America's biggest scandals.

VISION, MISSION, VALUES: CULTURE'S TRIUMVIRATE

Behind every good company culture stand strong vision, mission, and values statements. A company's vision, mission, and values not only express long-term goals and the plan for reaching them, but also tell employees how to behave when carrying out objectives.

Theodore Hesburgh, priest, educator, and former president of the University of Notre Dame, said, "The very essence of leadership is that you have to have vision. You can't blow an uncertain trumpet."

A vision statement outlines an organization's long-term goals and key objectives, and it provides direction to employees. A strong vision statement guides business strategy, unites employees, and focuses on the future.

Example: Microsoft—A personal computer in every home running Microsoft software.

Management consultant, educator, and author Peter Drucker said, "The mission says why you do what you do, not the means by which you do it."

A mission statement tells employees, shareholders, and customers *why* the organization exists. To that point, mission statements are as different as the companies behind them. According to Fred David, author of *Strategic Management: Concept and Cases*, all good mission statements focus on present "customers; products or services; markets; technology; concern for survival, growth, and profitability; philosophy; self-concept; concern for public image; and concern for employees."

Example: Bristol-Myers Squibb Company—To discover, develop and deliver innovative medicines that help patients prevail over serious diseases.

American film writer and producer Roy Disney said, "It's not hard to make decisions when you know what your values are."

A values statement outlines an organization's deeply held beliefs and tells employees how to behave while carrying out the company's vision and mission. Values are reflected in everything an organization does and are visible to those inside the organization as well as those outside. It tells you how an organization has acted in the past, how it acts in the present, and how it plans to act in the future.

Example: Toyota—Here are the company's core values:

Respect for the Law. Toyota Industries is determined to comply with the letter and spirit of the law, in and outside of Japan, and to be fair and transparent in all its dealings.

Respect for Others. Toyota Industries is respectful of the people, culture, and tradition of each region and country in which it operates. It also works to promote economic growth and prosperity in those countries.

Respect for the Natural Environment. Through its corporate activities, Toyota Industries works to contribute to regional living conditions and social prosperity and also strives to offer products and services that are clean, safe, and of high quality.

Respect for Customers. Toyota Industries conducts intensive product research and forward-looking development activities to create new value for its customers.

Respect for Employees. Toyota Industries nurtures the inventiveness and other abilities of its employees. It seeks to create a climate of cooperation, so that employees and the company can realize their full potential.

Interestingly enough, Enron's value statement was "Communication, Respect, and Integrity." It's short, succinct, and probably looked good on the company letterhead. Someone likely spent hours refining it. But employees didn't heed it because they couldn't hear it over the din of Enron's corrupt company culture—a culture that was strongly supported by Enron's incentive compensation system, which was designed to reward its best employees but was focused nonetheless on short-term earnings. To maximize bonuses, employees started deals, regardless of cash flow or profits. They were also rewarded for meeting the expectations of Enron's investors and of Wall Street, which encouraged them to record accounting results prematurely and to find creative ways of hiding the company's debt.

WHEN MOTIVATION FUELS CUSTOMER ANNOYANCE & ALIENATION

Recently while on an Alaska Air flight from San Francisco to Seattle, I was annoyed by the flight attendants' efforts to sign passengers up for Alaska Air credit cards. Not only did they pitch the credit cards over the loudspeaker a few times, but they also approached passengers individually. Trapped on a plane and trying to relax before an important meeting, I wasn't impressed with the hard sell, so I asked a flight attendant why she was pushing the card so relentlessly. She shared that Alaska Air flight attendants receive a $50 bonus for every passenger who enrolls on the flight.

Since I run a company focused on incentives and motivations, I wasn't surprised by her answer. But there is such a thing as *too much motivation*. When your employees are so driven by the promise of a bonus that they disregard their first duty to customers—in this case, the flight attendants' responsibility to keep passengers calm and happy—your incentive plan has backfired.

FOUR STEPS TO A DYNAMIC COMPANY CULTURE

Organizational vision, mission, and values don't build themselves. Here are four steps you can take to use data and your incentive compensation plan to fine-tune your messages and make sure everyone is singing the same tune.

Step 1: Evaluate. Your Company's Data Is Your Magic 8 Ball.

Look at your vision, mission, and values statements and make sure they are up to date and complement current organizational goals. If you haven't paid attention to these statements lately and need to refine them, get going.

Next, assess your current company culture. For the most part, you can do this by examining employee behavior. You'll know something is wrong with your company culture when employee actions don't complement your intended values. The best clues about your current company culture are found in historical and current data, which tell you everything you need to know about organizational processes and the people who support those processes.

For example, let's say that your organizational values promote teamwork, openness, and sharing, and your organizational goals are best supported by a culture that is collaborative. If employee actions and behaviors don't represent those values and goals,

FLATTENING THE HOCKEY STICK WITH SPIFs

Conventional B2B wisdom dictates that most deals close at the end of the quarter, with a cluster of them right before the cutoff point. If you were to chart the dates of closed deals on a graph and draw a line connecting each, your drawing would resemble a hockey stick.

It's therefore not surprising that when we took a look at when most of our deals were closing at Xactly we noticed a trend: Most of our larger customers (and larger deals) were waiting until the end of the quarter to make purchases, hoping, we assumed, to get the best deals from reps anxious to make quota.

In an effort to avoid the end-of-quarter rush, we then moved our fiscal year from the end of December to the end of January. We predicted that larger customers would still buy in March, programmed to think it was the end of the quarter and they were getting the best possible deals. We were excited to see the curve resemble a hump instead of the hockey stick. But this attempt to "flatten the hockey stick" didn't work. Instead of continuing to close the majority of sales in March, reps simply took more time with deals and pushed customers to close in April.

So instead of manipulating our deadlines, we decided to focus on motivating our sales reps better at key times by offering periodic SPIFs. For instance, one recent SPIF gives reps double credit toward membership in our President's Club for every deal they close in the first month of the quarter, motivating them to sell *sooner* rather than later. Because for ambitious reps there's prestige in being in this club—winners get to hang out with the top brass, and their professional stock goes up as their colleagues see they've been recognized—this is a killer bonus.

In order for SPIFs to effectively motivate, make sure they are never predictable. If your reps start to expect the same SPIF to be available next month, the month after that, and so on, they won't try as hard to achieve sales goals *now*. At Xactly, we introduce SPIFs sporadically and rarely use the same incentive twice. As a result, when we announce a new SPIF, we're usually rewarded with extra zeal from our sales team.

We've been more successful in flattening the hockey stick with positive incentives than we were with changing our deadlines, and along the way we learned a valuable lesson: Our reps, not our customers, drive the timing of closed deals.

and instead reveal an environment that is hypercompetitive and focused on individual success—that is, one in which employees are constantly undermining one another, stepping on one another's toes, and jockeying for position—you've got a problem. Not only is this type of environment unpleasant to work in, but if organizational success depends on collaboration, it's unlikely you'll meet your goals. Unfortunately, many employees—from leaders all the way down to entry-level employees—aren't aware that workplace issues result from a misalignment of values and behavior because values aren't communicated effectively. Many simply don't have a handle on what their organizational values *are*.

If data indicates that your company's true culture is not aligned with your intended culture, start talking to your employees. At the next staff meeting, sales retreat, or business planning session, take a few minutes to ask employees questions such as, *Who are we? What do we stand for?* and *What makes us who we are?* If you don't like their answers, if what you hear is at odds with the values you are trying to promote, or if employee responses aren't united—for example, if answers from departments differ, or if the answers of managers differ from the answers of sales reps—you're not sending a clear message about your organization's values.

Step 2: Articulate. Crank Up the Convo with Compensation.

Vision, mission, and values statements are supposed to support a company culture that results in success. But, as I mentioned earlier, employees often don't hear what you're trying to say. One of the best ways to crank up the volume, articulate your intentions, and make sure employees get the message is through your incentive compensation strategy.

Ask yourself these two questions:

What do I want to accomplish?

What compensation strategy will articulate my expectations to employees?

An incentive compensation plan that supports your intended culture:

Tells employees what is expected; and

Tells them how they are supposed to meet expected goals.

According to *CFO* magazine's 2012 Global Business Outlook Survey, the average company spends anywhere between 40 and 70 percent of its operating budget on employee compensation.[6] Designed incorrectly, your compensation strategy can break the bank. Aligned with company goals, it can increase the likelihood of your success.

Forget one-size-fits-all plans. Specific incentives should be tailored to specific individuals, communicating *exactly* how each individual should contribute, and how those contributions support the achievement of company goals. Those in sales support may be compensated very differently from sales reps, who are compensated differently from sales managers. Each targeted compensation plan should result in specific behaviors and actions. But *all* should drive the organization's intended values and culture.

For example, let's say you're introducing a new product line and looking for innovative start-up types who are willing to take risks. The compensation plan you design for reps in this group may include a smaller salary and stock options, resulting in higher bonus potential, and may vary considerably from the incentive compensation plans of sales reps working on your industry-leading, bread-and-butter product. While each compensation plan would encourage different behavior, both of them should still align with core company culture.

To figure out how well you're using compensation to communicate, look at your data. If individuals, teams, and the company as a whole are meeting goals with behaviors that align with your stated values, you're right on track. If, on the other hand, goals aren't being met, you have high turnover, or employee actions in general aren't to your liking, you may need to do a better job of using compensation to drive values and corporate culture.

Finally, if you're having a hard time attracting the right employees, take a long look at how you portray incentive compensation externally. In 2009, Kristine Kuhn, professor in the Department of Management at Washington State University, conducted a study to determine the effect of job ads on applicants' perception of company culture. When ads suggested that employees would be rewarded for individual performance or skill, applicants were more likely to perceive an organization's culture as individualist. But in cases where ads suggested that individuals were compensated with profit sharing, applicants were more likely to view company culture as collectivist.[7]

The moral of the story: If your organization is more likely to succeed with individualists, make sure your compensation plan doesn't shout collectivist, or vice versa.

Step 3: Reciprocate. Do Unto Others . . .

In 2002 Dell Computer issued a new corporate values statement, which it called "The Soul of Dell." In this statement, it articulated the five values that Dell considered imperative to its success: customer loyalty, teamwork, direct communication, relationships, global citizenship, and winning.[8]

What's interesting about this is that Dell's leaders didn't lock themselves in a room and write this definition alone, or even in one day. Instead, they engaged every single employee in the reexamination of company culture. The process took two years.

A company with a motivating culture doesn't just dictate that culture. Instead, company leaders find out what is important to employees. Using data, they determine what kind of culture and rewards resonate best with employees and then develop strategies that deliver on both counts. Organizations routinely expect employees to meet their expectations. In turn, a company that can meet employees' expectations is a great place to work.

Step 4: Investigate. Keep up with Ch-Ch-Changes.

According to the Society of Human Resources Management, about 30 percent of mergers fail because of culture incompatibility.[9] Perhaps one of the most famous culture clashes occurred between Daimler and Chrysler in the late 1990s. Though Daimler chairman Juergen Schrempp predicted a "merger of equals," it didn't take long for the two sides to collide. They argued about relatively small things, such as where to headquarter, as well as the most serious thing—how to operate the business.[10] The U.S.-based Chrysler complained that Germany-based Daimler was dominant and dishonest, and employee satisfaction flagged. By 2001 the value of the business had dropped significantly. Six years later, in 2007, the marriage was officially declared over when Daimler *gave* Chrysler to private investment firm Cerberus Capital Management, along with $675 million![11]

Company culture is not static. Whether your organizational culture has been affected by a large external event, such as a merger, or a smaller internal event, such as a change in leadership, it's important to take frequent looks at both culture and compensation to make sure they are still aligned.

By drilling into your data, you can tell whether you're still on track, whether employees are meeting your expectations, and whether your incentive compensation policies are meeting their expectations. Once that's done, you can adjust your compensation plan so that it supports the kind of culture your employees demand and meets your organizational goals.

―――――――

Now that you know the importance of aligning compensation with company culture, you're poised to unleash dramatic changes in employee satisfaction, performance, and company-wide results. In the next chapter, you'll learn how to use specific reward strategies to send your sales reps the kind of messages that influence objective-oriented behavior.

Visit www.GameThePlan.com to watch videos that share how to apply this chapter's principles in your own company.

CHAPTER 8

USING YOUR COMP STRATEGY TO UNLEASH MOTIVATED BEHAVIOR

At this point, you understand the importance of incentives and the link between motivational strategies and behavior. You know *why* it's important to align incentive compensation with company goals: namely, to see to it that employees engage in the types of behaviors that will help you reach your objectives. Now, let's get into exactly *how* you do that.

Many of the organizations I deal with subscribe to "best practice" incentive compensation strategies, using plans that have worked for their competitors or for others in their industry. But as I've said previously, an incentive compensation plan that isn't structured specifically for your organization isn't going to get you where you need to go unless you get very, very lucky.

Think of it this way: If you want to take your family on a ski vacation, making sure you end up in the mountains and not at the beach takes a lot more than packing your skis and hopping on a

plane. You need to figure out exactly where you're going, then plan
a detailed itinerary that enables you to get there—and only there. If
you neglect to carefully plan all of the legs of your travel, you could
end up anywhere!

Your incentive compensation strategy holds the key to inspiring the "right" employee behaviors. Many organizations get caught
up in the amount of money sales reps take home, competing with
other organizations by matching their base salary and commission
structures or by offering "better" incentives as a way to attract,
retain, and motivate top talent.

Yes, money is a key factor, but the mix of your compensation
components is even more important than that sole incentive. How
your company structures and balances incentives tells employees
exactly how to act. When incentives are used incorrectly, employee
behavior may be at odds with intended goals and organizational
values. But when incentives are used correctly, you can unleash the
type of motivated behavior necessary to catapult your organization
to the top.

"A" FOR EFFORT OR "F" FOR FAIL?

Michael, a consultant at a company that sells B2B software, has a
compensation plan that includes a twice-yearly bonus calculated from
four factors:

1. How much profit the company made in that six-month
   period

2. How much revenue Michael brought in during the same
   time frame

3. The hours Michael accrued

4. A subjective grade on overall performance with clients,
   awarded by Michael's boss

Michael was a confident rep, a star performer who always hit his targets. He was used to getting 100% of his bonus every six months. During one bonus period, however, he uncharacteristically made a few errors with an account and lost the deal. When it came time for his review, he entered his review expecting to receive a low bonus.

But, to Michael's surprise, even though his boss gave him a less-than-perfect grade on his job performance, his bonus was actually *more* than it would have been had he hit his target. His sub-par grade was offset by high company profitability and recognition of the additional hours Michael had put in to make up for his flubs. As a result, he walked out of his review with a 115% bonus.

The outcome of this compensation formula definitely worked in Michael's favor, and perhaps even cemented his loyalty to his company, but the fact that he earned such a healthy reward for not-so-great performance begs the question of whether the plan worked as well for his company. This is a great example of a company that needs to revisit its compensation strategy to make sure it's delivering a win-win for both parties.

TIME TESTED: TRIED-AND-TRUE INCENTIVES

When designing incentive compensation plans, companies use four main types of pay incentives.

The Base Salary: Your Home Run Maker

Base salary is the fixed amount paid to employees in exchange for work performed. In my experience, base salary is often viewed as the redheaded stepchild of the compensation world. Plan designers tend to ignore it, erroneously believing that of all the components in a rep's compensation mix, base salary speaks most softly. Therefore, they research the base salaries of reps at similar companies, come up with a competitive figure, and quickly move on to other incentives—even though keeping pace with others in the industry doesn't help a company meet objectives and goals.

What a mistake! *All* incentives—even base salary—have the ability to speak loudly. For example, a base salary that is in line with industry practices but that makes up 80 percent of a sales rep's overall compensation plan may result in a rep who isn't particularly hungry. A base salary that makes up only 20 percent of the overall compensation plan, however, may not attract the type of experienced talent you're looking for. On the contrary, it may attract entry-level salespeople who aren't ideal for the job.

Base salary can be used to convey important messages, as long as you think less about the actual figure and more about how it fits into the overall mix.

A Near-Sighted Strategy That Pays: Short-Term Incentives

If you view your base salary as one of the more tedious components of your incentive compensation plan, your short-term incentives become the life of the party. Every organization has short-term needs, and this type of incentive is the perfect vehicle for ensuring that those needs are met.

Short-term incentives are designed to build immediate energy and motivation for an organization's short-term goals. For example, if a sales leader wants reps to focus on a specific product launch within a specific deadline, he may design a contest that features short-term incentives to spur enthusiasm and shift focus.

Short-term incentives can run for a day, a week, or even a month or two, but they are best aligned with simple, immediate goals. One of the great things about short-term incentives is their flexibility: They can be used on entire teams that are united in one goal, or they can be used on one rep who needs an extra push.

Types of short-term incentives include:

- Cash bonuses

- Non-monetary incentives, such as recognition awards, weekend escapes, and gift certificates

- Work-life balance incentives, including time off or work-from-home privileges

- Nontraditional incentives, such as discount programs, extended wellness programs, and debit cards that fund education

GET PROACTIVE AND OPEN THE FLOOD "GATES"

When former rivals Quaker State and Pennzoil merged in 1998, they were tasked with building one solid team from two. Before the merger, most of the reps from both companies had focused on one or two product lines only. After the merger, they were expected to sell many varieties of motor oil as well as other automobile add-on items, such as air fresheners, tire cleaners, and so forth.

Because margins on add-ons are higher than those on oil, Pennzoil–Quaker State wanted to motivate its reps to amp up the sale of its many other ancillary products. Problem was, the automotive store buyers were focused on oil, and so the reps were simply selling more oil to those customers. To solve this problem, the company got proactive with a unique incentive strategy. They created "gates," that is, minimum levels of sales on particular add-on products that reps were required to meet before they could achieve higher commissions on their motor oil sales. The new gates created a huge shift in the reps' attitude toward selling add-ons, and Pennzoil–Quaker State's margins went up overnight.

The Midterm Incentive March

Midterm incentives typically comprise bonuses and commissions, and they are the primary vehicles used to tell sales reps what the company wants them to accomplish in the next month or the next quarter. Typically, a rep's quota is tied to midterm incentives. If you view short-term incentives as the life of the party, your midterm incentives become those that guarantee that the life of the organization marches forward at a steady pace.

IF YOU HAVE TO FEED IT, IT'S NOT A BONUS

Creative bonuses can show an employee just how much she means to you. But when creativity isn't combined with good judgment, imaginative bonuses can send the opposite message. Truth is, indeed, stranger than fiction!

One of Xactly's sales leaders talked to a woman we'll call Melanie. Her role included handling the booth at trade shows. At one such show, her company's booth was outfitted with Peanuts-themed paraphernalia. Dissatisfied with mere cartoon imagery, the CEO sent an assistant on a madcap mission to secure a purebred Snoopy look-alike that would be sold after the show. But the beagle gimmick backfired.

The puppy was terrified by the noise and the crowd, and Melanie was horrified by her boss's glib attitude toward the animal. When the trade show was over, the CEO couldn't sell the Snoopy impersonator as planned, so he decided to give it to Melanie with his blessing. "You seem to get along with the dog really well, and we were planning on giving you a bonus anyway, so the dog is yours to keep."

Whoa!

To her dismay, Melanie found herself being offered a puppy in lieu of a quarterly cash bonus! Though she wanted cash, she felt awkward saying so.

Fortunately, this story has a happy ending: Melanie spent many happy years with the dog, and she eventually moved on to a job where she was appreciated and rewarded with more appropriate bonuses!

Long-Term Incentives: For the Revenue Visionaries

Long-term incentives are used to incent behavior that promises the organization's long-term success. This type of incentive can be cash awards, based on the achievement of long-term goals, or can come in the form of stock options, restricted stock with time vesting, and performance shares.

Long-term incentives are great at encouraging behaviors that result in sustained company performance, and they are also effectual in attracting and retaining rock star reps. Because most long-term incentive programs vest over a longer period of time, they can be used to make sure that your best reps stick around and aren't wooed by competitors willing to pay a bit more short-term cash.

HOW ONE COMPANY HAS LOST ONLY THREE EMPLOYEES IN 15 YEARS

When it comes to employee management, longevity is a priority. Turnover is expensive, and valuable long-term employees have time-tested experience. BWSI, a Phoenix-based staffing company, has seen only three employees leave for greener pastures in over 15 years. Matthew Kinsey, the company's executive VP of research and development, explains how BWSI created a bonus structure that *retains* and *motivates* top employees:

> We set aside a significant portion of our gross profit and divide it up among the employees every quarter, but we escrow part of the bonus each quarter in case we have a bad quarter later on—which we haven't, yet—and then pay out the escrowed amount later with the Christmas bonus.

> We generally don't give raises in the first few years unless an employee takes on significantly more responsibility. But every quarter, each employee gets a bonus based on how well the company does overall. By using bonuses

> instead of raises to control labor costs, we keep our fixed
> overhead down. The ownership mantra here is that when the
> company does well, we all do well. And when the company
> doesn't do well, we don't have to worry about furloughs or
> cutting salaries!
>
> BWSI's savvy compensation strategy keeps employees motivated
> and on board, and it creates a strong correlation between company
> success and compensation payout. Rewarding for results keeps top
> performers hungry and committed.

BECOME A MIX MASTER

If you want your incentive plan to work, you'll need to carefully balance your design choices. Missteps can cause the wrong employee behavior. So, before you blame your employees for things gone wrong, take a close look at your plans and the messages they send.

All too often, sales managers and plan designers balance incentives in ways that have worked in the past—in previous years, at other companies, or with other teams—expecting to get the same results. But a plan that worked for another company might have mixed results at yours. Your goals may be completely different, your business may be in a different phase, or your sales team may have a different demographic.

For example, let's contrast Company A—a company in its growth phase, with a rapidly expanding product line—with Company B—a start-up. To promote more immediate growth at Company A, the incentive compensation plan may be heavy on short- and midterm incentives but light on long-term incentives. This plan might be a slam-dunk, but it probably will not serve the needs of cash-strapped

Company B, which needs to incent reps to sell their hearts out now but can't pay them until later.

CREATIVE INCENTIVES THAT CREATE EVEN MORE CURRENCY THAN CASH

Reps love cash bonuses, but sometimes a creative, non-cash perk can bring out your sales team's friendly competitive spirit just as well.

For example, consider the sales manager who compiled a list of prospects from a trade show. He wanted to find a new way to inspire his team to act on the leads. His reps already received their usual bonuses from booked business, but as an extra perk, this manager offered a rare bottle of wine from his personal collection to the rep who could generate the most activity from the new list.

The wine was worth about $100, which when translated to cash wouldn't have made for a very inspiring incentive. But the one-of-a-kind prize held clout, and the reps clamored to get their hands on this special bottle.

That's the power of incentives. Done right, they create even more currency than cash. Rewarding reps with prizes that carry emotional value doesn't just motivate them; it also helps build a healthy sense of competitive team spirit. The personal touch can go a long way in managing a sales team.

Sometimes, a tried-and-true incentive compensation plan simply stops working, leaving managers and plan designers scratching their heads, wondering what's up. Both internal and external changes can necessitate a shift in your incentive compensation plan. It's important to review plans frequently, to figure out what's working and what isn't, and to change the plan if you're no longer getting what you want.

At other times, what seems to be a thoughtfully designed incentive compensation plan inspires the exact opposite behavior you are looking for. Which leads me to . . .

THE SEVEN DEADLY SINS OF INCENTIVE COMPENSATION

In his highly entertaining and very popular paper "On the Folly of Rewarding A, While Hoping for B," Stephen Kerr gives example after example of organizations that—despite good intentions—inadvertently reward discouraged behaviors with poorly designed compensation plans, while failing to reward desired behaviors.[1]

In one example, Kerr tells the story of an insurance company that rewarded accuracy in paying surgical claims by tracking the number of returned checks and letters of complaints that agents received. Because underpayments were likely to result in complaints, and overpayments were—obviously—happily accepted, employees adhered to the "when in doubt, pay it out" adage. The intent of the compensation plan may have been to improve accuracy, but its true message was "keep customers happy." In the meantime, the organization was very *unhappy* when it realized employees were paying claims that perhaps should not have been paid.

If the compensation plan you've designed isn't motivating employees and boosting your bottom line, you may be committing one of the seven deadly sins of incentive compensation.

BETTER DRIVING, HIGHER MARGINS

Sales reps aren't the only team members whose activity can be influenced by a smart compensation strategy. For food companies, product value and profit are directly tied to freshness, distribution speed, and product handling, so it makes sense to motivate drivers for prompt and intact deliveries. (I apologize in advance if this example turns your stomach as it did mine!)

For one company that sells whole chickens to grocery stores and restaurants, delivery presented a particular challenge. Customers paid for chicken by weight, but that weight tends to decrease between the slaughterhouse and the store. In the chicken industry, there's an effect called "weepage": As slaughtered chickens are transported, parts can fall out of the bodies of the fowls, and thus the delivered product weighs less when it gets to the store than it did when loaded onto the truck.

To combat weepage, this chicken company decided to incent drivers to be extra careful when handling the chickens. They offered better compensation to drivers whose loads "wept" less, and the incentive worked. The chicken company made higher margins and less product was wasted.

Sin #1: Misalignment of incentive plan and business objectives

Are you sure, *really sure*, that your comp plan supports your objectives? For example, an incentive plan that features a bonus for hitting a quarterly number, with a kicker for sales closed after that, should, at first thought, result in maximum sales. But what are you really telling your sales team? If you don't adequately reward excellent performance in this quarter, you send reps a clear message to delay deals in order to receive quarterly bonuses.

IS YOUR INCENTIVE PLAN SAYING WHAT IT MEANS?

Design Component: High incentives

- What You Are Trying to Say: We want to attract and retain top reps and to encourage maximum sales.
- What Reps Might Hear: Sell at all costs, even if it means you win and the company loses.

Design Component: Incentives based on customer satisfaction

- What You Are Trying to Say: Keeping our customers happy is part of our long-term sales plan.
- What Reps Might Hear: Put customer happiness ahead of sales, even if it means the company loses profits.

Design Component: Monthly objective, with bonus

- What You Are Trying to Say: Sell consistently and as much as possible!
- What Reps Might Hear: Maximize commissions by selling every other month, or by hoarding sales.

Design Component: Incentives paid on units

- What You Are Trying to Say: The more you sell, the more you earn.
- What Reps Might Hear: Sell as many units as possible, at deep discounts if necessary, even if it means the loss of profits for the company.

Design Component: Team incentives

- What You Are Trying to Say: Working as a team is key to our company's success.
- What Reps Might Hear: Relax and let your teammates pick up the slack.

Design Component: Multiple metrics

- What You Are Trying to Say: There are so many ways for reps to make money!
- What Reps Might Hear: This incentive compensation plan is complex and difficult to understand. Ignore it!

When it comes to misalignment, the devil is usually in the details. If you're noticing undesirable behavior, take a closer look at what your incentive compensation plan might be saying.

Sin #2: Inability to trace data

The best incentive compensation plans rely on data from various systems. Critical among them are Human Capital Management (HCM), Enterprise Resource Planning (ERP), Configure/Price/Quote (CPQ), and Customer Relationship Management (CRM). Without traceability, it's difficult for the organization to tie sales rep behavior to their payments, to measure individual and company success, and to audit payments.

A transparent, traceable data system also allows for significantly better forecasting, so you can further build a compensation plan that complements your goals.

Sin #3: Lack of benchmarks

In order to determine if your incentive compensation strategies are working, it's important to use benchmarking, either against an aggregate group or industry standards, or self-benchmarking against goals established at the beginning of the year. Both forms of benchmarking can help you gather the data you need to identify variations from region to region, product to product, and sales rep to sales rep.

With this enlightening information in hand, you can compare sales incentives to sales performance and make sure that incentives are driving desired behaviors. For example, benchmarks can help you determine whether group- and team-based incentives are driving performance at other offices or competitors, or if they are encouraging slacking. Or, if benchmarks indicate that fluctuating measures are making quotas unattainable, you can introduce relative performance pay to keep thresholds meaningful.

Sin #4: Complex plans

Are your sales reps not responding to your incentive compensation plan the way you would like them to? It may be because they don't understand it. Reps who find your plan unduly complex will just ignore it. And when that happens, it's a sure bet their behavior isn't aligned with your intended goals.

As far as I'm concerned, an incentive compensation plan that contains six or seven components is a strong sign that leadership is weak and using the incentive compensation plan as another sales manager. If rep behavior is chaotic, check out the number of measurements. Xactly research indicates that a well-designed compensation plan should have no more than three measures.

Sin #5: Haphazard credit assignments

If your business is like most, you credit five or fewer people for each deal. But if you have a complex sales cycle, you might credit as many as thirty people. Some organizations with extremely complex sales cycles even credit more than one hundred people per sales deal!

When an organization doesn't have the data to track large numbers of people involved in a sales deal, it may take the easy way out and credit entire teams instead of individuals. In this situation, it's simply not possible to determine how the actions of your reps are impacting results.

Sin #6: Compensation plans that don't motivate

Sometimes, plan components designed to motivate employees in a certain way do anything *but* motivate.

Cases in point: At H. J. Heinz Company, bonuses were based on increased annual earnings. So, division managers gamed shipments and payments. At Sears, a compensation plan for auto mechanics designed to boost services resulted in the sale of unnecessary repairs, causing Sears to abolish its commission plan and close stores across California.[2] Certain types of elements, such as holds and releases, have too much time between action and reward to be truly motivating. Other elements, such as capped incentive plans, can also prevent sales reps from achieving their best. As a matter of fact, an American Management Association study showed that reps who were moved from a fixed bonus plan to an uncapped commission structure performed 24 percent better.[3]

Comparing your sales data to your intended goals can tell you whether a de-motivating compensation plan is hampering your success.

Sin #7: Accelerator issues

Some organizations use accelerators to motivate reps to sell more because, for the most part, they work. Accelerators that result in too many unexpected paycuts, however, can reduce profits. The result? Many people simply avoid them. Unfortunately, those who avoid accelerators miss out on the benefits they provide when used correctly.

There is but one way to ensure that your accelerators remain a friend, and not a foe: model.

Using your data, come up with solid answers to these three questions:

1. What do you expect sales performance to be?

2. What would happen if a couple of reps earned far more than expected?

3. What would happen if most reps earned far more than expected?

With answers in hand, you can adjust your plan to minimize your risk.

MASTER BALANCE IN FOUR STEPS

With the seven deadly sins in mind, how do you balance your incentives to (1) guarantee that your reps get the message and are motivated to act on it, and (2) ensure that when reps game the plan—and they will—everyone wins?

Again, there's no one answer. Balancing incentives simply isn't simple. But you can increase your odds of better balance by following these four steps:

1. Forecast demand and sales cycle length. Dig into historical data to determine which products are good candidates for shorter measurement periods, and which are not. That information will help you balance your short-term, midterm, and long-term incentives. One study found that a contact lens manufacturer, which had predictable product demand and quarterly commissions, increased revenues by 9 percent just by shortening measurement periods from one quarter to one month.[4]

2. Set up trackable, objective measures. You won't know if your incentive plan is working if you can't measure it. Review critical measurements, determine whether the timing works, and gauge behavior to determine whether it's in line with company goals. Then, make any adjustments to incentives necessary to create win-win situations.

PAY IT FORWARD, LITERALLY

Sales leaders of one computer hardware company noticed their compensation plan was causing a less-than-ideal trend. Though they paid bonuses quarterly, they did not reward reps for closed deals until the hardware was installed and the switch was turned on. As a result, service reps would scramble each quarter to install all the hardware before the close of the bonus period. This racked up overtime hours, which cost the company a lot of money.

This payout rule is common for hardware companies, but it makes for a sub-par compensation strategy. So this company decided to try another motivational tactic. To offset losses, the leaders added up the money typically spent on overtime, and offered proportional bonuses to reps who closed deals and installed the hardware in the first half of the quarter. As a result, one-third of the company's business was pulled forward.

3. Determine the cost of gaming the system. Review recent deals and take a long, hard look at your average deal profit margin in the final days of a term. In *The Cost of High-Powered Incentives: Employee Gaming in Enterprise Software Sales*, Ian Larkin says that tech companies typically lose anywhere between 6 percent and 8 percent of revenue because of compensation plan loopholes that reps have uncovered![5] Yep, you heard that right: between 6 percent and 8 percent of revenue! For example, reps with long sales cycles can delay deals to suit their commissions needs. An integrated data system can help you track this kind of behavior, thus enabling you to balance incentives so that rep wins don't equal company losses.

4. Think of the worst possible scenario. Look at past data to project potential sales, lay out your incentive plan, then ask yourself what would be the worst-case scenario if most of your reps gamed the plan and found every single loophole. If you lose when reps win, you need to better balance the mix of your incentives to mitigate risk. Remember, reps will game the plan! And if your plan is good, that shouldn't be a problem!

It used to be that you'd have to manage each of these four steps individually, calling upon many different sources of truth, from spreadsheets to email, to get the answers you need to balance your incentive compensation elements.

But as I've mentioned before, if you're still using spreadsheets you're putting yourself at a distinct disadvantage. Spreadsheets are filled out, stored, updated, and generally managed by people. As much as I like people, they are prone to error. If you're making decisions using erroneous information, you're probably not making the right decisions.

Thanks to technology, there's no need to use spreadsheets ever again. New solutions that use aggregated, anonymous data help organizations give their incentive compensation plans the deep scrutiny they deserve, so you make decisions that enable your strategy to fuel optimal performance and engagement.

———

Any employee will tell you that his or her paycheck is important. But the right mix of incentive compensation components is essential to driving the desired behaviors that guarantee your organization meets its objectives and goals.

In the next chapter, I'll show you how you can use years of accumulated big data on sales performance to deliver new intelligence and best practices to organizations of all sizes and industries. These terabytes of data can be sliced several different ways, enabling you to benchmark your current strategy and to see how it stacks up against top-performing companies in terms of plan design, business process workflow, and effective reporting. I'm also going to ask you to take a test to see how you currently stack up against everyone else. Once you have that data in hand, you'll be on your way to developing a winning incentive compensation strategy.

Visit www.GameThePlan.com to watch videos that share how to apply this chapter's principles in your own company.

CHAPTER 9

BENCHMARKING FOR BETTER INSIGHT— TO HIT RESULTS OUT OF SIGHT

A t this point, I hope we can all agree that data is the lifeblood of performance measurement. But it's the breadth and the depth of the *actionable insight* that data provides that counts most. In this chapter, I'll continue to talk about the transforming nature and importance of data in general, but I'll also refer to Xactly's specific data now and again, as we're currently the only company that offers the kind of data set needed to dive as deep as I'm going to ask you to dive.

For the record, this is a deeper dive than you've done before. Many organizations have looked to surveys and compensation consultants for answers to their comp questions. The reason leaders have shied away from better analysis is a historical lack of measurable, comparable, real-life data on incentive compensation management. But while the intentions behind relying on consultants and past experiences have been good, the answers that these approaches generate don't always yield the kind of personalized insight companies need. Self-reported surveys or surveys that are very limited don't have all of the information an organization needs to make informed, impactful decisions. For example, a survey might have been designed to solve problems that aren't of interest to a particular company, or its participant base might be too small, or even inappropriate in terms of industry, geography, or company size. Don't get me wrong; the work that consultants do is incredibly valuable, and you can't get their kind of expertise anywhere else. But it's really important that you augment their expert recommendations with the right data—and by that I mean data that's industry-specific, benchmarked, and actionably relevant.

Quite frankly, any ready-made survey you access is likely to have gaps between the information it offers and the information your company needs. Some companies, particularly those that have identified specific problems or want very particular questions answered, sponsor and run their own compensation surveys—a time-consuming, expensive undertaking. Without someone exceedingly experienced at the helm, they run the risk of getting erroneous, inaccurate, and unhelpful information, at best. At worst, they could violate antitrust laws and land your organization in hot water.

THE VARIABLE COMPENSATION CHALLENGE: FROM VISION TO ACTION

According to the 2012 World at Work Compensation Program and Practices Report, 84 percent of companies across all industries use variable compensation for non-sales. This does not include sales-specific variable compensation plans. Two years earlier only 80 percent of organizations used variable compensation pay.[1]

Today, more companies are jumping on the variable pay band-wagon as they begin to understand how it can be used to change behavior and drive results. When we explored the subject of how to motivate employees in earlier chapters, we learned this was a good move—a necessary move, even. But it doesn't come without its challenges. (Note that I said variable pay *can* be used to change behavior and drive results!) The use of variable compensation increases complexity, resulting in many more questions and more difficulty finding the answers.

In an attempt to rein in variable comp, some companies have automated the process. Automation tools are great for helping Finance prepare accurate, on-time payroll—especially when dealing with a workforce with different commission and pay structures—but historically, they haven't been able to give leaders the information needed to analyze current pay strategies against their peers, or to make strategic decisions based on industry vertical best practices.

The intent of any company introducing variable compensation is to maximize workforce motivation, so it's frustrating when it doesn't work. Variable compensation complexity and automated tools are just two of the dynamics driving down returns. As I just implied at the end of the last paragraph, the third dynamic driving down returns—and the focus of this chapter—is the current lack of data-driven, industry-specific benchmarks.

FOUR THINGS YOU SHOULD KNOW ABOUT REAL-TIME DATA

1. Long-term data facilitates long-term results. Xactly has gathered more than eight years' worth of empirical data, allowing those who access it valuable insight on employee performance and engagement.

2. The best incentives vary by niche. The terabytes of information we have collected can be sliced by industry, geography, or company size, enabling organizations to gather valuable intelligence about best practices.

3. Sales behavior can be standardized. Our well-organized empirical data can tell you how sales staff typically behaves in certain situations.

4. Visibility creates vision. Once empirical data sheds light on employee behavior, organizations can use this understanding to design incentive compensation plans that increase motivation, complement company goals, and improve business results.

Unleash Bigger and Better Insights

Automation makes life much easier at modern organizations, but it's far from perfect. On-premises solutions keep data in silos, where employees are unable to aggregate it, making it impossible to develop benchmarks. This obscures what leading organizations do differently from lagging companies and makes it impossible for companies to measure themselves against organizations at both ends of the spectrum. Without this information, it's nearly impossible to make educated, confident decisions that ensure that you are doing what you need to do to properly and effectively motivate performance in your organization.

Fortunately—and for the first time ever—a new 100 percent

cloud-based, multi-tenant compensation software solution enables companies to aggregate, anonymize, and analyze compensation data, then access all the information needed to maximize their own compensation investments. (This is where I might get a little self-promotional. Hey, it's hard not to be excited when you've got something this revolutionary on your hands.)

Just where does this data come from, and how much is there, really? To give you a short answer, eight years' worth. For eight years, Xactly has collected empirical performance data from hundreds of companies, hundreds of thousands of customer employees, more than a billion transactions per month, and approaching a trillion dollars in compensation payouts—all in an anonymous and aggregated model.

And now it's at your fingertips to tell you what to do.

BENCHMARKING FOR BALANCE

An organization can use Xactly Insights™ data to benchmark its sales compensation practices. It can compare the health of its organization to that of the anonymous organizations in the data set to determine whether or not its practices are in line with other best practices in plan design, business process workflow, and effective reporting. The unique, crowd-sourced data provides exceptional value.

When you're looking at hundreds of customers, thousands of compensation plans, hundreds of thousands of subscribers, and billions of credits over many years, you're not just looking at an unreliable snapshot in time, or at someone else's irrelevant comp stats. Instead, you're looking at terabytes of data that help you figure out how you stack up against your peers, so you can create incentive compensation plans that attract, engage, and retain your industry's top talent.

For example, our data shows that the most common compensation plan in the software technology industry relies on 75 percent of variable pay coming from first-year bookings, 23 percent of pay coming from backlog, and 2 percent of pay coming from services.

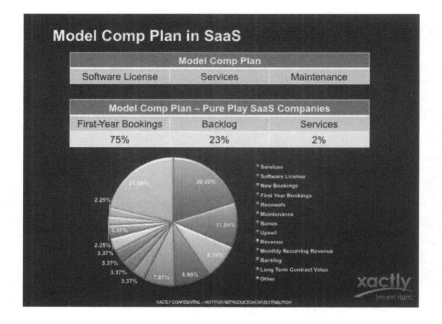

Benchmarks are segmented, providing very specific information:

- Strategic—Benchmarks relevant to strategic business planning

- Operational—Benchmarks that complement core business practices, such as compensation administration and compensation design

- Financial—Benchmarks that support financial planning, budgeting, accounting, and modeling

- Adoption—Benchmarks that help our customers improve their data quality, allowing them to take advantage of other Insights™ capabilities

With benchmarking, you can balance the elements in your favor so you get the results you want and need. You can also use the data to answer questions you've been asking for years, such as these:

- How should I structure the base vs. variable pay mix?

The mix of base and variable pay should be largely unique, based on your organization's demographic and what drives individual employee needs. As I noted in previous chapters, some generations are motivated by the stability of a higher percentage of base pay, while other generations are motivated by immediate rewards, prizes, or competition.

Benchmarking lets you compare your compensation mix to other companies in your industry, in your area, or that are of comparable size, enabling you to gain insight into how companies at all performance levels are structuring compensation. Once you see how you stack up—that is, once you figure out what you're doing right and what needs to be improved—you can make informed changes to your compensation strategies that have been proven, through data, to improve other businesses' bottom lines, and therefore position your company for similar boosts. A relatively minor adjustment to the mix of your compensation elements can yield big results, and it can mean the difference between employees who regularly kill it and employees who race to get out the door at five o'clock.

- How should I handle quota timing? Should I pay monthly? Quarterly? Annually?

Quota timing, as well as short and long measurement periods, can impact results.

A study at Stanford University, for instance, showed that sales increased as sales reps got closer to quota.[2] I have first-hand experience with this, as I describe in chapter seven in the sidebar titled "Flattening the Hockey Stick with SPIFs." When Xactly shifted its fiscal year by one month, ending it on January 31 instead of December 31, revenue spikes also shifted. This told me not only that the distance to quota had an influence on the sales profile but also that we could control spikes through thoughtful compensation strategies.

Take a look at your own data and then look at the data of best-in-class companies. You'll find that monthly or year-to-date quotas with good accelerators for deals signed early will give reps plenty of incentive to meet, and even exceed, quotas. In addition, data shows that quick commission payments—those received at the end of the month for work done at the beginning—also control revenue spikes.

- Am I capping profits when I cap commissions?

Commission caps are typically used to control spending, or when leaders are worried about reps making more than managers do. Capping might seem like a good idea under those circumstances, but our data shows that only about one-third of reps meet 120 percent or more of their target incentives. The incentive attainment bell curve (see the section titled "Step Up to the Insights™ Challenge and Find Out How You Stack Up" that follows) shows a spike at 100 percent, with drop-off occurring as the percentage of quota attained climbs. In other words, if you cap your plans, you're telling your reps to put on the brakes at a certain point. And that point could be well below what your reps are capable of reaching.

The takeaway from this data is that you're totally in control of whether your reps reach for the sun or settle for landing on the moon. A good rep will go only where you tell her to go, and no further.

- Am I paying too many people per deal?

Lots of companies have no idea how many people they pay per deal or order. When they find out, they're absolutely astonished. Xactly has one client that pays 161 people for every deal! You don't need to be brilliant to understand that this extreme example is a bad practice. But what about all the companies that are paying, say, thirty people per deal? For most, it's still a bad practice. Think about it for a second: If you're a chief sales officer and you're spreading a certain amount of money among thirty people, how many of them are you really motivating? (And how unhappy is your CFO with you?)

Xactly Insights™ looks at data from companies at all performance levels to determine how many people paid per deal is too many. The verdict? According to data gathered from the highest-performing companies in our database, the ideal number of people credited per transaction is five.

If you're paying more than that, take a look at your own data to see who really influences a deal and how, and then make cuts and adjustments so your credits make more sense.

- How many measures should I include in my plan?

There's no doubt that measures align compensation with company objectives, drive sales performance, and reward outcomes. So it's tempting to want a gazillion of them. But

GIVE YOUR ENTIRE SALES TEAM 20/20 VISION —WITH ONE TOOL

Strategic incentives can motivate your sales reps to prioritize selling products that add the most to your company's bottom line.

Optimum Lightpath, a division of Cablevision, operates a fiber-optic network throughout the most heavily inhabited parts of New York, New Jersey, and Connecticut. If one of its sales reps sells Optimum Lightpath's service to a modern, cable-ready building that's already wired for Internet—called a "lit" building in industry parlance—the service can be turned on with a simple flip of a switch. Understandably, Optimum Lightpath makes a higher profit margin on servicing those buildings. When it comes to older buildings that aren't wired, of course, the company has to send technicians out to provision and set up the fiber-optic technology, which is vastly more expensive.

It made sense for Optimum Lightpath to motivate its sales reps to prioritize selling to lit buildings, but for a long time the company was handicapped because it used spreadsheets to track its incentive compensation. It needed to keep its strategy simple because it didn't have the infrastructure for the complexity of multiple commission rates. All reps were paid the same commission rate, regardless of whether they sold to lit buildings or those that needed to be wired. The downside of this strategy? Reps weren't motivated to seek out deals with higher margins.

Optimum Lightpath solved this problem by investing in automated compensation tools that allowed it to create different incentive rates for different types of sales. Now a rep who closes a deal with a lit building gets a higher commission rate, and both that rep and Optimum Lightpath experience higher profits as a result.

Matt Grover, VP of sales operations at the time the new automated compensation system was put in place, was thrilled with the change. "We don't have to water down our programs anymore, but can instead align them closely with corporate objectives and achieve new business agility."

By making the shift to automated compensation tools, Optimum Lightpath gained the ability to be strategic with its incentive plan and align sales team behavior with business goals.

too many measures contribute to plan complexity (more on that in the next question). If reps don't know what to focus on, or if they don't understand your compensation plan, you can bet the plan will fail.

In addition to the challenge of finding the right measures for your sales compensation plan, you have to find the right number of measures. According to our data, leaders of the best-performing companies give their sales teams the best possible chances of succeeding when they limit their measures to three or fewer.

- How complex should my plan be?

Complexity comprises the number of measures an organization pays on, as well as the way an organization uses different types of compensation to drive different actions.

The more complex compensation plans become, the more they enter into a zone of high costs and low value, because they lack benchmarks and ease of use.

Our data shows that the more complex compensation plans are, the worse the company results. Keep in mind, though, that poor results can also reveal that your plan isn't complex enough. The key lies in the balance.

STEP UP TO THE XACTLY INSIGHTS™ CHALLENGE AND FIND OUT HOW YOU STACK UP

Xactly has developed an incentive compensation assessment that tells you how your incentive compensation plans, processes, and measurements stack up with those of the best of your peers, and other similar-sized companies in our database.

At the end of the assessment, companies are assigned to a quadrant—data driven, best in class, reactive, or process driven—that measures sales compensation value against process effectiveness. Companies are also assessed by category, and are given a yellow belt, a green belt, or a master black belt in plan design, business process workflow, and effective reporting and analytics.

The assessment, which can be downloaded at http://insightsassessment.xactlycorp.com, asks you to assess yourself in the following categories:

Plan Design

- Please enter the number of distinct sales variable commission plans in use.

- How many unique commission plan components are in use in your organization?

- Please select the average number of components in your plan.

- What is your primary plan component?

- What is your secondary plan component?

- How many sales roles do you have that are paid variable compensation?

- Please select the average number of people credited per sales transaction.

YOU CAN'T CLAW BACK A YACHT

American International Group (AIG) is a multinational insurance corporation with over 63,000 employees. They have many long-term accounts, called "House Accounts," that never have to be serviced. Technically, the company policy is to assign House Accounts to managers, who do not receive commissions on the low-maintenance clients. However, it used to be common practice at AIG for managers to play favorites and assign those accounts to reps on the down-low, allowing them to get commissions without ever having to talk to the clients.

This was a great setup for the reps, of course, who were making a lot of money on House Accounts and, as a result, buying big-ticket items like yachts and jets. But it wasn't a great setup for AIG. The company was bleeding money but couldn't put its finger on the gash. Finance didn't have insight into what was happening until Xactly implemented its automated compensation management system. Once the system provided AIG with easy access to reports detailing rep compensation, company leaders were shocked to see how much money they were losing on these sly commissions.

AIG tried to claw back the money they'd lost to reps, but the cash had already been spent on luxury items. AIG learned an important lesson in a very expensive way

- How many quotas do you have per plan?

- What is the frequency of your primary quota?

Compensation Administration

- What percent of your reps make quota?

- What percent of revenue do you pay in sales variable compensation?

- Do you leverage survey data or external reports for plan design?

- Do you leverage compensation consultants to design your plans?

- How often do you review plan effectiveness?

- How many commission transactions do you process per period?

- Approximately what percentage of total variable compensation spent goes to discretionary or out-of-plan exception payments?

- On average, what percentage of your sales reps are affected by manual adjustments each month?

- Please select the average number of days from the sales transaction to the commission payment.

- Approximately how many commission-related errors does your sales comp team handle per month?

- Is the current source data that is input to the sales comp system certified data from business systems such as ERP, CRM, etc.?

Analytics and Benchmarking

- How many source systems do you leverage to calculate variable sale compensation?

- What department does sales comp administration report to?

- What's your annual sales team turnover?

- How frequently do you calculate sales variable compensation?

- How long does it take to calculate sales variable compensation per period?

- Do you currently report on sales compensation ROI by sales rep and sales manager (ratio of revenue generated to sales compensation paid)?

- Do you track and benchmark sales compensation ROI by territory/region/organizational unit?

- Do you track and benchmark sales compensation ROI by product?

- Do you track and benchmark sales comp expenditures by type (salary, plan, bonus, discretionary, SPIFs)?

- Can you track and benchmark attainment of sales reps vs. quota/target/objective?

- What is your typical variation between budgeted and actual commission payments?

- Can you tie all of the commission payments back into their specific source transaction?

- Do you use external data sources to benchmark your sales compensation performance?

Once you've answered the assessment questions, we'll email you a benchmark report—an evaluation of your current sales compensation capabilities according to plan design, business process workflow, and effective reporting and analytics.

———

Data is the foundation of performance measurement. While we've historically relied on comp consultants and surveys to drive our decisions, these methods have left some questions unanswered. Fortunately, new technology that enables us to access industry-specific, relevant, benchmarked data means we can now design incentive compensation plans that drive desired results.

In the final chapter, I'll highlight the main points I hope you take away from this book.

Visit www.GameThePlan.com to watch videos that share how to apply this chapter's principles in your own company.

CHAPTER 10

THE BEST-GAMED PLANS: SOME FINAL THOUGHTS

When you picked up this book, its title may have led you to believe it was about showing sales managers and compensation plan designers the wily ways in which sales reps game incentive compensation plans, with tips on how to prevent such behavior.

Initially, you might have been surprised to learn that I accept and advocate gaming the system. Now, many pages later, you might be *really* surprised to find that you—yes, you—are beginning to embrace the idea of your reps exploiting every loophole that exists in your own incentive plan.

How could that be? Because now you better understand the nuances of human motivation; realize that aligning your compensation plan with organizational goals will drive the kind of behavior you're looking for; and know that if you have a good incentive compensation strategy, gaming the system has one result—a win-win situation for your reps and for your company.

But before you begin to design the best-gamed plan, I want to leave you with these important reminders.

It's not *all* about the money, honey. If you've learned one thing about motivation from this book, it should be that although money is a great incentive, it's not the ultimate one. Be sure to do your homework and offer a competitive base salary and commission structure, and then do even *more* homework to figure out what else motivates your staff. As a general rule of thumb, all people crave recognition, so make sure that your incentive compensation strategy includes plenty of opportunity for your reps to earn your praise and recognition. Beyond that, the answer to what motivates your employees will vary among groups and even among individuals, depending upon the generations from which members of your sales force hail. For example, the incentives that motivate Baby Boomers will be very different from those that motivate Millennials.

Don't reinvent the wheel. If your current incentive plan isn't working, don't completely scrap it and try something new without figuring out why it failed in the first place. When Thomas Edison was hard at work on the electric lightbulb, he famously said, "I have not failed. I have just found ten thousand ways that do not work." Analyze your data to find ways that haven't worked, and then use what you learn to develop more successful incentive compensation plans.

Understand your audience. Remember, the sales reps you incent today are different from the reps you've incented in the past. Make an effort to understand generational differences between reps and how those differences affect incentives;

thereafter, customize incentives based on your reps' cultural influences, needs, and desires. A critical component of this process is digging into your data to see if your incentives are truly speaking to your sales force. If data shows that you're not getting the behavior you want, you either don't fully understand your audience or you haven't done a good job of tailoring incentives to that audience.

GETTING FOX-Y WITH INCENTIVES

Companies can (and do) tell the world both how and why they trump their competition. But in this age of social media, those messages carry a lot more weight with potential customers when they come from a friend. Member of Generation Y in particular are far more likely to take action—buy a product, donate to a cause, write a review—when a request comes from their peers.

Xactly launched a loyalty and gamification platform, Friends of Xactly (FOX), to encourage customers to become evangelists. FOX members earn points for social media follows, customer referrals, taking our mascot Quota on vacation, and other activities and challenges. Points are redeemable for Xactly merchandise, gift cards, and the ultimate prize: dinner with me.

In the first year alone, the FOX program delivered some impressive results:

- Drove more than 80% of customer activity on the Salesforce AppExchange, resulting in a 2012 Customer Choice Award.

- Lit up our LinkedIn page with recommendations, follows, and shares, making it one of LinkedIn's 12 Best Company Pages of 2012.

- Ignited social interaction in minutes. From one simple advocate challenge, we gained 89 Twitter followers and 96 Facebook likes.

Don't try to be too smart. You have read a lot of examples of good intentions gone awry. Don't play incentive compensation like a complicated game of chess, assuming that if you make one particular move your reps will make another. Instead of relying on what you *think* might happen, use your data to forecast what *will* happen. Remember that compensation plans can produce the exact *opposite* response that you want if you don't take the time to consider what your plans are really telling reps. The messages you think your plans are sending may be completely different from the messages they actually are. Let your data help you design incentive compensation plans that say what you mean.

Know how many people you pay for each deal. Are you paying dozens of people for one deal? Hundreds? That's okay, as long as each person is actually contributing to it and being compensated in a way that complements their contribution. Review the data in your incentive compensation system to determine exactly how many people you are paying per deal, how much you're paying them, and if they contribute to the deal. Don't waste your valuable and limited dollars paying too many people for each deal. If you're paying someone who isn't contributing, cut that person loose from the group of people being paid.

SPIFs are an important part of the program. The business world is constantly changing, and the most successful organizations are able to adjust their compensation plans quickly to react to changing market conditions. One of the best ways to react to these external changes, without completely revamping your incentive plan, is to introduce SPIFs. SPIFs are terrific tools for influencing rep behaviors to make sure that short-term goals and needs are met.

CUSTOMER SERVICE THAT ACTUALLY SELLS

Bank tellers are typically paid on salary or by the hour because they're considered customer service. But leaders of one southern U.S. bank, MidSouth, have a different philosophy. They know that anyone interfacing directly with customers has the potential to influence customer wallet-share, so they consider their tellers to be sales reps of sorts.

As members of the bank's welcoming committee, tellers offer customers friendly smiles and become familiar faces to many; they answer basic questions about banking and direct customers to resources within the bank, including the loan agents.

MidSouth is focused on increasing its wallet-share, so motivating tellers to learn more about the loan programs to best direct customers to agents makes a lot of sense. MidSouth offers a ten dollar SPIF to tellers each time they connect a customer to an agent.

Why not take advantage of this setup and better incent your front-line players?

Remember, people change . . . And their compensation plans should change as well. Just because a plan has worked for a particular rep in the past is no guarantee that it will work in the future. People's lives, expectations, needs, and levels of engagement fluctuate for a variety of internal and external reasons. In my experience, organizations have two typical reactions when a former rock star rep begins to underperform: (1) They ignore the situation, or (2) they dangle poorly reasoned incentives before the person in the hope the rep will find his fire. In reality, if a rep's behavior has changed, it's an indication that your current incentive plan, for whatever reason, isn't working. It's time to use your data to figure out what specific changes need to be made to increase motivation.

Competition can be healthy. It's not only okay to show reps how they stack up to their peers, but doing so can be incredibly motivating. Make rep progress public knowledge by posting leaderboards, sending email blasts, and holding awards ceremonies and recognition events. Develop gamification tactics and sales contests with desired prizes that encourage reps to compete against one another. When you dole out the goodies, make sure you do so publicly. The best sales reps are competitive by nature, so if you include an element of "winning," your organization is likely to win as well.

Transparency is critical. Don't wait until the end of the month or the end of the quarter to show your sales reps how they're doing.

PLAYING TO WIN . . . MONEY, NOT GLORY

Sales reps tend to love sports, and that's no surprise, because both reps and athletes are driven by competition.

In the fall of 2012, Xactly flew six SPIF winners to Detroit to see the Giants play the Tigers in Game 4 of the World Series. The anticipation leading up to this once-in-a-lifetime event drove great performance among our reps, many of whom are big baseball fans.

Like sales reps, athletes and their team managers are regularly offered incentives to perform better: Contracts are negotiated to offer players and managers more money for more wins. For instance, a baseball manager might get a bonus if his team goes to the World Series, and a quarterback might get a bonus if he's voted MVP of the Super Bowl.

Likewise, any sales rep will tell you that she plays for money, not glory.

As for the Tigers vs. the Giants, our San Francisco Bay Area–based home team won Game 4 of the series, sweeping the Tigers and making this SPIF an extra valuable bonus.

Give them constant access and insight into their progress, like with a "Show Me the Money" button in their sales compensation tool. Your data system can be configured to tell reps everything from how many units they've sold and how close they are to reaching their quotas to how much they'll earn in commission in certain scenarios. Letting them know where they are *at any given moment* tells them what they need to do to meet their—and your—goals. Showing sales reps how close they are to quota, and what they stand to make when they close deals, can give them the extra motivation they need to keep pushing.

KISS and sell up. In other words, keep it simple, smarty-pants. When it comes to evaluating rep behavior and goals, keep tabs on the number of measurements you include in your incentive compensation plan. If you have too many measures, your reps will become confused, unfocused, and won't know what you want them to sell. The best messages are sent through simple, finite measurements that are easy to track and understand. Xactly empirical data shows that, as a general rule, there should be no more than three measures. If the number of measures creates confusion or lack of understanding, your reps will simply ignore your plan! And if they ignore your plan, they won't be able to help your organization meet its goals.

If you're using spreadsheets and your competitor isn't, you're at a major disadvantage. Spreadsheets are prone to error and they simply can't supply you with the single source of truth you need to gather accurate information and make informed decisions. According to CSO Insights' 2010 Sales Compensation Performance report, 70 percent of companies using automated sales compensation systems report that their plans generally drive the precise selling behavior they desire, as compared to 57 percent of companies using manual or spreadsheet-based solutions.[1]

THE POWER OF PERCEPTION

One of our early clients, Ironport Systems, Inc., sold products that protected enterprise companies against security threats and spam. As a young tech start-up, Ironport had to find its way when it came to properly motivating sales reps. In the beginning, if two reps shared a deal, the company created a split, offering each rep a percentage of the commission. Often this split was an even 50-50, but in certain cases one rep would get a higher cut, say 60%, if he had seniority over the other rep. Needless to say, splitting the commissions this way caused some bad blood between reps.

So Ironport altered its compensation strategy and began to pay every sales rep involved in a deal 100% of the commission. To afford this, the company lowered the reps' commission amounts so that the ultimate payout stayed pretty much exactly the same. In the past, a $1,000 commission split 50-50 would have earned each rep $500. With this shift in the compensation strategy, each rep was now receiving 100% compensation on each deal—but 100% compensation was now $500. Even though the reps were making more or less the same amount of money, the perception that they weren't sharing commissions led to a major attitude adjustment.

Reps were a lot happier, and Ironport was eventually acquired by Cisco in a deal valued at $830 million! Clearly, Ironport was doing something right.

Analyze and change your plans. Your business isn't static, so your incentive compensation plan shouldn't be either. Analyze and change your plans each year. Access your data to determine how well your incentive compensation plans are driving desired behavior. Then, figure out how you might be able to change the mix of your compensation elements to get even better results. Your incentive compensation data system will tell you everything from revenue per sales rep to how much your organization is making per deal. It will then use predictive modeling to tell you such important revelations as how much you need to pay a rock star rep to prevent her from quitting, the impact of a particular compensation plan on productivity, or how changes in compensation will affect profits.

Embrace variable compensation. Variable compensation creates win-win situations for reps and for the organization. When you hear horror stories about incentive compensation plans gone wrong, or if you can tell your own, just remember that win-lose situations are a result of bad plans. Period. The thoughtful use of variable compensation is one of the *best* tools to drive desired behaviors and get your message across. Don't be afraid of variable compensation. Use predictive modeling to determine outcomes, measure progress frequently, and fine-tune your plans when your data shows it's time.

Build trust and confidence. One of the best ways to build trust and confidence is to pay accurately and consistently. Paying correctly not only saves your organization money and fosters good relationships between Sales and Finance, it also ensures that your reps trust the organization. And trust is a key component in attracting, engaging, and retaining top talent.

And last, but without a doubt the most important . . .

Gaming the plan is a good thing. It really is! As long as you've aligned compensation with your company goals and your incentives carry a strong message and drive the right behavior, any win for your rep will result in a win for the organization. Let your reps game away, and enjoy the benefits!

To the win-win!

Visit www.GameThePlan.com to watch videos that share how to apply this chapter's principles in your own company.

NOTES

Chapter 1

1. Ancient Roman Economy. unrv.com. Retrieved from www.unrv.com/economy.php.

2. Leeson, Peter T. 'An-*arrgh*-chy: The Law and Economics of Pirate Organization." *Journal of Political Economy*. December 1, 2007. Retrieved from http://www.peter_eeson.com/an-arrgh-chy.pdf

3. Ibid.

4. Ibid.

5. Ibid.

6. The Daily Kos. "Battle of the Bunnies." K.A. Muston. July 26, 2009. Retrieved from http://www.dailykos.com/story/2009/07/26/757919/-BATTLE
-OF-THE-BUNNIES

7. The History Guide. "Lectures on Modern European Intellectual History. Napoleon's Proclamation to His Troops in Italy (March-April 1796)." Retrieved from www.historyguide.org/intellect/nap1796.html

8. PBS, "Campaigns and Battles: First Italian Campaign 1796-7." Retrieved from PBS.org/empires/napoleon/n_war/campaign/page_1.html

9. Napoleonic Guide. "Legion of Honour." Retrieved from www.napoleonguide.com/legionorg.htm

10. Smiley, Gene. Marquette University. "The U.S. Economy in the 1920s." March 26, 2008. Retrieved from http://eh.net/encyclopedia/article/smiley.1920s.final

11. Cooley, Thomas. "The Soaring Twenties." *Forbes*. July 29, 2009. Retrieved from http://www.forbes.com/2009/07/28/great-depression-roosevelt-hoover -opinions-columnists-thomas-f-cooley.html

12. Nickell, Joe. "Peddling Snake Oil." *Investigative Files*. Vol. 8.4, December 1998. Retrieved from www.csicop.org/sb/show/peddling_snake_oil/

13. Lindard, Laura. "Birth of the American Salesman" *Harvard Business Review*. April 19, 2004. Retrieved from hbswk.hbs.edu/item/4068.html

14. Shook, Robert L. *The Greatest Sales Stories Ever Told: From the World's Best Salespeople* (McGraw-Hill, 1997).

15. Ibid.

16. Cooley, Thomas. "The Soaring Twenties." *Forbes*. July 29, 2009. Retrieved from http://www.forbes.com/2009/07/28/great-depression-roosevelt-hoover

    -opinions-columnists-thomas-f-cooley.html

17. Frymdan, Carola and Saks, Raven E. "Executive Compensation: A New View from a Long-Term Perspective, 1936–2005." Oxford University Press, 2010. Retrieved from http://web.mit.edu/frydman/www/trends_rfs2010.pdf

18. Ibid.

19. Maslow, A.H. "A Theory of Human Motivation." *Psychological Review* 50.

20. Ibid.

21. "Executive Perquisites—What 2012 Proxy Statements Have Revealed." *Ayco Compensation & Benefits Digest*. Vol. XX, Issue VI, June 15, 2012. Retrieved from www.aycofinancialnetwork.com/news/digest/digest_1206.pdf

22. Rajan, Raghuram and Wulf, Julie. "Are Perks Purely Managerial Excess?" National Bureau of Economic Research (NBER) Working Paper No. w10494, May 2004.

23. "National Survey Reveals Americans Prefer a Night in Jail to Losing Job Benefits." *PR Newswire*. November 15, 2012. Retrieved from www.prnewswire .com/news-releases/national-survey-reveals-americans-prefer-a-night-in-jail-to-losing-job-benefits-179465381.html

24. Brox, Denise. "14 Companies with Incredible Employee Perks." Salary .com. Retrieved from www.salary.com/14-companies-with-incredible -employee-perks/slide/2/

25. Hall, John. "The Unique Job Perks that Employees Love." *Forbes.* November 28, 2012. Retrieved from www.forbes.com/sites/johnhall/2012/11/28/the -unique-job-perks-that-employees-love/

26. Hastings, Reed. "How to Set Your Employees Free." *Bloomberg Business Week.* April 12, 2012. Retrieved from www.businessweek.com/articles/2012-04-12 /how-to-set-your-employees-free-reed-hastings

27. "10 Perks We Love." John Cuneo, Inc. Retrieved from www.inc.com/ss/10 -perks-we-love#6

28. Ibid. Retrieved from www.inc.com/ss/10-perks-we-love#9

29. "A Statistical Profile of Employee Ownership." *The National Center for Employee Ownership.* February 2012. Retrieved from www.nceo.org/articles /statistical-profile-employee-ownership

30. Edmonston, Peter. "Google's I.P.O., Five Years Later." *New York Times. Deal-Book.* August 19, 2009. Retrieved from dealbook.nytimes.com/2009/08/19/ googles-ipo-5-years-later/?_r=1

31. "Employee Stock Options Fact Sheet." *The National Center for Employee Ownership.* Retrieved from www.nceo.org/articles/employee-stock-options -factsheet

Chapter 2

1. Howard, Bill. "Tesla Model S is Now the Best-Selling Luxury Car—with an Asterisk." *ExtremeTech.* May 15, 2013. Retrieved from www.extremetech.com/ extreme/155897-tesla-modle-s-is-now-the-best-selling-luxury-car-wth-an -asterisk

2. Lawler, Ryan. "Tesla CEO Elon Musk Says He Got Into the Electric Car Business Because No One Else Would." *TechCrunch.* May 29, 2013. Retrieved from techcrunch.com/2013/05/29/elon-musk-d11

3. Goodman, Peter S. "Jobless Rate at 14-Year High After October Losses." *New York Times.* November 7, 2008. Retrieved from www.nytimes.com/2008/11/08 /business/economy/08econ.html?pagewanted=all&_r=0

4. Deal, Jennifer J., Sarah Stawiski, and William A. Gentry. "Employee Engagement: Has It Been a Bull Market?" Center for Creative Leadership. July 2010. Retrieved from www.ccl.org/leadership/pdf/research /EmployeeEngagement.pdf

5. Schroeder-Saulnier, Deborah D. "Mgt. Working Well: A Priority for Engaging Employees and Driving Productivity." Right Management 2010. Retrieved from www.right.com/thought-leadership/e-newsletter/working-well-a-priority-for-engaging-employees-and-driving-productivity.pdf

6. Lunsford, Seleste. "Survey Analysis: Employee Motivation by Generation Factors." *AchieveGlobal*. December 2009. Retrieved from www.slideshare.net /EileenDuffy/achieveglobal-survey-results-motivation-by-generation-factors

7. Lyman, Amy. "Nordstrom—Great Service for Over 100 Years, Best Company for 25 Years." Great Places to Work Institute 2009. Retrieved from resources .greatplacestowork.com/article/pdf/2009-best-company-for-25-years -nordstrom.pdf

8. Pearce, Keith. "Intel's Seventh Inning Stretch: 8-Week Paid Sabbaticals." Intel blog. December 3, 2009. Retrieved from blogs.intel.com/jobs/2009/12/03 /intels_seventh_inning_stretch_8_week_paid_sabbaticals

9. Deal, Jennifer. *Retiring the Generation Gap: How Employees Young and Old Can Find Common Ground* (Jossey-Bass, 2006).

10. Casserly, Martyn. "What is Big Data? Understanding Big Data, and How It Affects Us All." *PC Advisor*. April 24, 2013. Retrieved from www.pcadvisor .co.uk/features/tech-industry/3443835/what-is-big-data

11. Laney, Doug. "3D Data Management: Controlling Data Volume, Velocity, and Variety." Meta Group. File 949. February 6, 2001. Retrieved from blogs .gartner.com/doug-laney/files/2012/01/ad949-3D-Data-Management -Controlling-Data-Volume-Velocity-and-Variety.pdf

12. Cukier, Kenneth and Mayer-Schonberger, Viktor. *Big Data: A Revolution that Will Transform How We Live, Think, and Work.* (Eamon Dolan/Houghton Mifflin Harcourt, 2013).

13. "Computer Associates to Restate Earnings." *Associated Press*. May 27, 2005. Retrieved from www.nbcnews.com/id/8008515/#.Um3LxiT0NqM

14. "Better Tools, Better Process, Better Performance: Best-in-Class SPM Deployments Mirrored by Xactly Customers." Aberdeen Group. May 2013.

Chapter 3

1. "Engagement at Work: Its Effect on Performance Continues in Tough Economic Times." Gallup. 2013. Retrieved from www.gallup.com /strategicconsulting/161459/engagement-work-effect-performance-con-tinues-tough-economic-times.aspx

2. "Employee Engagement Eroding, Says Mercer 2012 Survey." Staff. American Society for Training and Development. October 10, 2012. Retrieved from www.astd.org/Publications/Blogs/Workforce-Development-Blog/2012/10 /Employee-Engagement-Eroding-Says-Mercer-2012-Survey

3. Kruse, Kevin E. *Employee Engagement 2.0: How to Motivate Your Team for High Performance* (CreateSpace Independent Publishing Platform, 2012).

4. 2012 Global Workforce Study. "Engagement at Risk: Driving Strong Performance in a Volatile Global Environment." Towers Watson. Retrieved from towerswatson.com/assets/pdf/2012-Towers-Watson-Global-Work -force-Study.pdf.

5. "Engagement at Work: Its Effect on Performance Continues in Tough Economic Times." Gallup 2013. Retrieved from www.gallup.com/strategic consulting/161459/engagement-work-effect-performance-continues -tough-economic-times.aspx

6. Boushey, Heather and Glynn, Sarah Jane. "There are Significant Business Costs to Replacing Employees." Center for American Progress. November 16, 2012. Retrieved from www.americanprogress.org/issues /labor/report/2012/11/16/44464/there-are-significant-business-costs-to -replacing-employees/

7. "Want to Retain Me? U.S. Workers Say 'Show Me the Money.'" Randstadusa .com. October 2, 2012. Retrieved from www.randstadusa.com/about-ranstad /press-room/want-to-reatin-me-us-workers-say-show-me-the-money

8. "Better Tools, Better Process, Better Performance: Best-in-Class SPM Deployments Mirrored by Xactly Customers." Aberdeen Group. May 2013.

9. Murphy, Mark. Leadership IQ 2013. "Job Performance Not a Predictor of Employee Engagement: New Analysis Linking Engagement Scores with Appraisal Scores Shows Low Performers More Engaged Than Middle and High Performers."

10. Schindlholzer, Berhard. "Defining Strategic Stretch Goals to Stimulate Innovation in Organizations." Customer Experience Academy. November 24, 2008. Retrieved from http://www.cxacaademy.org/defining-strategic-stretch-goals-to-stimulate-innovation-in-organizations.html

11. Donald, Brooke. "To motivate many Americans, think 'me' before 'we,' say Stanford psychologists." Stanford Report. January 28, 2013. Retrieved from news.stanford.edu/news/2013/January/motivation-independence-psychology-012813.html

12. Blodget, Henry. "Google Gives All Employees Surprise $1,000 Cash Bonus and 10% Raise." *Business Insider*. November 9, 2010. Retrieved from www.businessinsider.com/google-bonus-and-raise-2010-11

13. Dewhurst, Martin, Guthridge, Matthew and Mohr, Elizabeth. "Motivating People: Getting Beyond Money." *McKinsey Quarterly*. November 2009. Retrieved from www.mckinsey.com/insights/organization/motivating_people_getting_beyond_money

14. Steenburgh, Thomas and Ahearne, Michael. "Motivating Salespeople: What Really Works." *Harvard Business Review*. July-August 2012. Retrieved from hbr.org/2012/07/motivating-salespeople-what-really-works/ar/1

15. Morath, Eric. "Labor Department: Error Could Cause 3 Quarters of Compensation Data to Be Wrong." *Wall Street Journal Blogs*. April 30, 2013. Retrieved from blogs.wsj.com/economics/2013/04/30/labor-department-error-could-cause-3-quarters-of-compensation-data-to-be-wrong/

16. Krugman, Paul. "The Excel Depression." *New York Times*. April 18, 2013. Retrieved from www.nytimes.com/2013/04/19/opinion/krugman-the-excel-depression.html?_r=0

17. "Better Tools, Better Process, Better Performance: Best-in-Class SPM Deployments Mirrored by Xactly Customers." Aberdeen Group. May 2013.

18. Charles, Erik. "Too Many Pans in the Fire? For Performance Measures, Less Means More." *Xactly Blogs*. February 5, 2013. Retrieved from http://www.xactlycorp.com/media/2013/02/for-performance-measures-less-means-more/

19. "Better Tools, Better Process, Better Performance: Best-in-Class SPM Deployments Mirrored by Xactly Customers." Aberdeen Group. May 2013.

20. Makin, Simon. "To Predict Success In Children, Look Beyond Willpower." *Scientific American*. March 11, 2013. Retrieved from www.scientificamerican .com/article.cfm?id=to-predict-success-children-look-beyond-willpower

21. Kanter, Rosabeth Moss. "Ten Reasons People Resist Change." *Harvard Business Review Blog Network*. September 25, 2012. Retrieved from blogs.hbr .org/2012/09/ten-reasons-people-resist-change

22. "Better Tools, Better Process, Better Performance: Best-in-Class SPM Deployments Mirrored by Xactly Customers." Aberdeen Group. May 2013.

Chapter 4

1. Stump, Scott. "He Did It! Daredevil Nik Wallenda Wire Walks Across the Grand Canyon." *Today News*. June 23, 2013. Retrieved from www.today .com/news/he-did-it-daredevil-nik-wallenda-wire-walks-across-grand-6C10411621

2. Cardinal, Ken and Florin, Beth. *Conducting Compensation and Benefits Survey* (World at Work Press, 2012).

3. Prendergast, Canice John. "What Happens Within Firms? A Survey of Empirical Evidence on Compensation Policies." University of Chicago Press, January 1998.

4. Ariely, Dan, Gneezy, Uri, Loewenstein, George, and Mazar, Nina. "Large Stakes and Big Mistakes." Federal Reserve Bank of Boston Working Papers No. 05-11, July 23, 2005. Retrieved from www.bostonfed.org/economic/wp /wp2005/wp0511.pdf

5. Zoltners, Andris A. and Sinha, Prabhakant. "Sales Territory Alignment: A Review and Model." *Management Science*. Vol. 29, No. 11, November 1983.

6. Zoltners, Andris A. and Lorimer, Sally E. "Sales Territory Alignment: An Overlooked Productivity Tool." *Journal of Personal Selling & Sales Management*, Vol. 22, No. 3, Summer 2000. Retrieved from http://www.kellog.northwester.edu /faculty/zoltners/htm/pdfs/zoltners_final.pdf

7. Tognazzini, Ryan. "Quota Attainment: The Panic-Euphoria Continuum." *Sales and Marketing Effectiveness Blog*. May 8, 2011. Retrieved from http://www .salesbenchmarkindex.com/bid/49877/Quota-Attainment-The-Panic -Euphoria-Continuum

8. Hayes, Erin. "Google's 20 Percent Factor." *ABC News*, May 12, 2008. Retrieved from abcnews.go.com/Technology/story?id=4839327

9. Bishop, Bryan. Apple Encourages Employees to Work on Personal Projects Under 'Blue Sky' Program." *The Verge*. November 12, 2012. " Retrieved from www.theverge.com/2012/11/12/36337786/apple-blue-sky-program -employees-personal-projects

Chapter 5

1. Boushey, Heather and Glynn, Sarah Jane. "There are Significant Business Costs to Replacing Employees." Center for American Progress. November 16, 2012. Retrieved from www.americanprogress.org/issues /labor/report/2012/11/16/44464/there-are-significant-business-costs-to -replacing-employees

2. Retrieved from www.googlepleasehire.me

3. CFO Concerns. What are the Top Challenges Facing Today's Financial Executives? Robert Half 2011.

4. American Society of Training and Development Staff. "$156 Billion Spent on Training and Development." December 6, 2012. Retrieved from www.astd .org/Publications/Blogs/ASTD-Blog/2012/12/156-Billion-Spent-on- Training-and-Development

Chapter 6

1. Briscoe, David. "It's Harder to Go to Work, Report Says: Job stress: U.N. study points to growing evidence of problems around the world where companies are doing little to help employees cope with the strain of modern industrialization." *Los Angeles Times*. April 4, 1993. Retrieved from articles.latimes .com/1993-04-04/news/mn-19037_job-stress

2. "Work Organization and Stress-Related Disorders." Centers for Disease Control and Prevention. NIOSH Program Portfolio. Retrieved from www.cdc .gov/niosh/programs/working/risks.html

3. Ibid.

4. "Stress in America 2009." American Psychological Association. Retrieved from www.apa.org/news/press/releases/stress-exec-summary.pdf

5. "Stress in America." American Psychological Association. October 24, 2007.

6. "Fact Sheet By the Numbers." Psychologically Healthy Workplace Program. American Psychological Association Practice Organization. 2010. Retrieved from www.apa.org/practice/programs/workplace/phwp-fact-sheet.pdf

7. "Job Openings and Labor Turnover Survey Highlights." U.S. Department of Labor Bureau of Labor Statistics. July 2013.

8. Palmer, Alex. "Money Not a Top Motivator." *Incentive*. August 30, 2012. Retrieved from www.incentivemag.com/Incentive-Programs/Engagement/Articles/Study--Money-Not-a-Top-Motivator/

9. British Library Management & Business Studies Portal. Retrieved from www.apa.org/pubs/info/reports/2007-stress.doc

10. Ibid.

11. Taylor, Frederick Winslow. *The Principles of Scientific Management*. (Cosimo Classics, 2006).

12. Ibid.

13. Judge, Timothy A., Piccolo, Ronald F., Podsakoff, Nathan P., and Shaw, John C. "The Relationship Between Pay and Job Satisfaction: A Meta-Analysis of the Literature." *Journal of Vocational Behavior*. Vol. 77, No. 2, October 2010. Retrieved from http://www.timothy-judge.com/Judge,%20Piccolo,%20Podsakoff,%20et%20al.%20%28JVB%202010%29.pdf

14. Gross, Jessica. "What Motivates Us at Work? 7 Fascinating Studies that Give Insights." *TED Blog*. April 10, 2013. Retrieved from blog.ted.com/2013/04/10/what-motivates-us-at-work-7-fascinating-studies-that-give-insights/

15. Ariely, Daniel. "What Makes Us Feel Good About Our Work?" TEDTalk filmed October 2012. Retrieved from http://www.ted.com/talks/dan_ariely_what_makes_us_feel_good_about_our_work.html

16. Ariely, Dan, Kamenica, Amir, and Prelec, Drazen. "Man's Search for Meaning: The Case of Legos." *Journal of Economic Behavior and Organization*. January 17, 2008. Retrieved from http://people.duke.edu/~dandan/Papers/Upside/meaning.pdf

17. Ryan, Richard M. and Deci, Edward L. "Self-Determination Theory and the Facilitation of Intrinsic Motivation, Social Development, and Well-Being." *American Psychologist*, Vol. 55, No. 1, January 2000.

18. LaBarre, Polly. "What It Takes to Do New Things at Work, Overnight." CNN Money. March 22, 2012. Retrieved from http://management.fortune.cnn .com/2012/03/22/what-it-takes-to-do-new-things-at-work-overnight/

19. Lapowsky, Issie. "10 Things Employees Want Most." *Inc. Magazine*. August 27, 2010. Retrieved from http://www.inc.com/welcome.html?destination=http:// www.inc.com/guides/2010/08/10-things-employees-want.html

20. "The Frustrated Employee: Help Me Help You." Hay Group. Retrieved from http://www.haygroup.com/downloads/ww/misc/frustrated_employee _4pp_%28singles%29.pdf

Chapter 7

1. Blacksmith, Nikki and Harter, Jim. "Majority of Workers Not Engaged in Their Jobs." Gallup. October 28, 2011. Retrieved from http://www.gallup.com /poll/150383/majority-american-workers-not-engaged-jobs.aspx

2. Peck, Sara. "The Best Workplace Luxuries Anywhere." *Forbes*. August 6, 2010. Retrieved from http://www.forbes.com/2010/08/06/office-perks -luxuries-leadership-careers-best.html

3. Watkins, Michael. "What Is Organizational Culture? And Why Should We Care?" *Harvard Business Review*. May 15, 2013. Retrieved from http://blogs .hbr.org/2013/05/what-is-organizational-culture/

4. Reckard, E. Scott. "Wells Fargo Accuses Workers of Opening Fake Accounts to Meet Goals." *Los Angeles Times*. October 3, 2013. Retrieved from http: //articles.latimes.com/2013/oct/03/business/la-fi-1004-wells-fargo -firings-20131004

5. Sims, Ronald R. and Brinkmann, Johannes. "Enron Ethics (Or: Culture Matters More than Codes)." *Journal of Business Ethics*. Vol. 45, No. 3, July 2003.

6. Duke University/CFO Magazine Global Business Outlook Survey. December 2012. Retrieved from http://www.cfosurvey.org/13q1/PressRelease.pdf

7. Kuhn, Kristine. "Compensation as a Signal of Organizational Culture: The Effects of Advertising Individual or Collective Incentives." *The International Journal of Human Resource Management*. Vol. 20, No. 7, 1634–1648, July 2009.

8. Fisher, Lawrence M. "How Dell Got Soul," *strategy+business*. Fall 2004.

9. *SHRM Case Study: Culture Management and Mergers and Acquisitions.* Society for Human Resource Management. March 2005. Retrieved from http://www.shrm.org/Publications/hrmagazine/EditorialContent/Documents/CMS_011564.pdf

10. Jamieson, Bob. "DaimlerChrysler Merger a Fiasco." *ABC News.* January 25. Retrieved from http://abcnews.go.com/WNT/story?id=131280&page=1

11. Edmonson, Gail. "Daimler Gives Chrysler to Cerberus." *Bloomberg Business Week.* May 14, 2007. Retrieved from http://www.businessweek.com/stories/2007-05-14/daimler-gives-chrysler-to-cerberusbusinessweek-business-news-stock-market-and-financial-advice

Chapter 8

1 Kerr, Stephen. "On the Folly of Rewarding A While Hoping for B." *Academy of Management Executive.* Vol.9, No.1.

2. Baker, George, Gibbons, Robert, and Murphy, Kevin. "Subjective Performance Measures in Optimal Incentive Contracts." *Quarterly Journal of Economics.* 109-1125-56, 1994.

3. "Motivating Your Sales Force: Do Bonuses or Commissions Work Better?" *PR Newswire.* July 9, 2013. Retrieved from http://www.prnewswire.com/news-releases/motivating-your-sales-force-do-bonuses-or-commissions-work-better-214742031.html

4. Misra, Sanjog and Nair, Harikesh. "A Structural Model of Sales-Force Compensation Dynamics: Estimation and Field Implementation." Stanford University Graduate School of Business Research Paper No. 2037. Simon School Working Paper No. FR 09-26. 2010.

5. Larkin, Ian. Harvard Business School. February 20, 2013. *The Cost of High-Powered Incentives: Employee Gaming in Enterprise Software Sales.* Retrieved from http://www.hbs.edu/faculty/Publication%20Files/13-073_cbb24c28-9e84-47d9-8a32-f01b73cfda13.pdf

Chapter 9

1. "World at Work." Compensation Program and Practices 2012. Retrieved from http://www.worldatwork.org/waw/adimLink?id=65522

2. Misra, Sanjog and Nair, Harikesh. "A Structural Model of Sales-Force Compensation Dynamics: Estimation and Field Implementation." Stanford University Graduate School of Business Research Paper No. 2037. Simon School Working Paper No. FR 09-26. 2010.

Chapter 10

1. CSO Insights, 2010 Sales Compensation and Performance Report.

INDEX

ABOUT THE AUTHOR

Christopher W. Cabrera is a thought leader and expert in sales performance management, incentive compensation, and employee motivation. Since founding Xactly Corporation in 2005, he and the firm have received many accolades. Chris was chosen as the 2011 Alumni Entrepreneur of the Year by the Lloyd Greif Center for Entrepreneurial Studies at the University of Southern California's Marshall School of Business. Xactly was named to the *Wall Street Journal*'s "Next Big Thing" list in 2012 and 2013, and was recognized as a Great Place to Work® in 2012.

Chris advises a number of start-up companies, and he speaks regularly at industry conferences and at Stanford, the University of California at Berkeley, USC, and Santa Clara University. He is on the board of USC Marshall Partners, Northern California, and on the advisory board for SCU's Leavey School of Business as well as the SCU Center for Innovation and Entrepreneurship. He and his wife, Marla, have been married for 23 years, and they have two children, Alexa and Cole.

47204035R00139

Made in the USA
San Bernardino, CA
24 March 2017